The Backyard Boatyard

To Ruth

Contents

	List of Illustrations	ix
	Preface	xi
1/	The Float	1
2/	Eyebolts and the Catwalk	10
3/	Docks and Docking Arrangements	17
4/	The Float Becomes a Barge	29
5/	A Gin Pole	39
6/	Unstepping Your Own Mast	46
7/	Cradles, Trailers, Marine Railways	58
8/	Haulout and Winterizing	74
9/	Storage Facilities	85
10/	Fitting Out	92
	Appendix A: A Proper Mooring Pendant	105
	Appendix B: Engine Maintenance	112
	Index	123

Illustrations

Figure		Page
1	Float	2
2	Float under construction	3
3	Float and catwalk	4
4	Float construction details	7
5	Deck of the float	8
6	Face piece for the float	9
7	Eyebolts and their installation	11
8	Shore end of the catwalk	13
9	Float end of the catwalk	14
10	Splicing a post for the dock	19
11	Dockbuilding the hard way	19
12	Ready for business	20
13	Winter ice on the Great Lakes	21
14	Dock construction, pile driver	22
15	Setting pilings	24
16	Dock and fender board	25
17	Bulkhead and bank details	27
18	Outboard and davit on the float	30
19	Float's winch, mooring, trip-line	31
20	Float rigged for hoisting	32
21	Motorized float	33
22	Mooring setup	35

Figure		Page
23	Mooring and racing buoy	36
24	Gin pole construction details	40
25	Hoisting the float	42
26	Float on the bank	42
27	Float descending the bank	43
28	Preparing float haulout	44
29	Old tractor motor	44
30	Motor as a winch	45
31	Skinning the gin pole	48
32	Details of the mast-stepping gin pole	49
33	Mast-stepping gin pole setup	50
34	Base of the gin pole	52
35	Pole resting on the dinghy	52
36	Pole cranked up	54
37	Mast being raised	54
38	Mast in position	55
39	Pole and mast stored	55
40	Mast dolly	56
41	Rugged cradle	59
42	Rugged cradle	60
43	Cradle iron-work details	61
44	Cradle for trailering	63
45	Trailer	63
46	Auto chassis used as a trailer	64
47	Converted horse trailer	65
48	Marine railway	67
49	Home-built railway	68
50	Cradle and rail	69
51	Haulout on marine railway	70
52	Haulout	71
53	Basic marine railway car	71
54	Rail in winter	72
55	Anchor fastening and punch	72
56	Bottom scrubber	76
57	Boat cover frame	81
58	Old boat shed	87
59	Lifeboat Station No. 7	87
60	Bosun's locker	88
61	Chart stowage	88
62	Sail and gear stowage	89
63	Dinghy hoisted to garage ceiling	90

Preface

This book is aimed at the person who wants to have the fun of rigging up his own gear and equipment to do boating jobs that might otherwise be light on pleasure and heavy on expense. It covers the season — from setting the mooring with a home-built gin pole and float, fitting-out and stepping the mast, to dock, bulkhead, and cradle building and finally to haulout, layup, and storage. All the devices in the book have two things in common. First (with a couple of exceptions, which are noted), they have been built and tried out — and they work. Second, they're inexpensive.

In reviewing the memories of 50 years around boats, I find that the important ones revolve around the grand waterfront types I've met, associated with, and worked for, the ones with whom I've sailed, cruised, raced, studied, taught, and dock-sailed. I wish to thank them all for their part in making this book possible — for the skills, ideas, and attitudes I've assimilated from them through the years.

Special thanks go to my brother Sid for permission to include descriptions of a number of his highly successful devices.

Howard Barnes
The Parrot's Roost

The Backyard Boatyard

1

The Float

While most of our boating has been done on fresh water, for the last dozen years, my wife and I have been saltwater sailors — resulting in some changes in our life-style. For one thing, instead of resting in a slip alongside a wharf, we lie to a mooring out near the mouth of a cove. After a season or so of doing without the convenience of a wharf, I decided to build a float. My brother Sid and I built one over at his place next door some years ago. He anchored his catwalk to a couple of eyebolts set into a ledge near shore, and this scheme worked out well, so I decided to do the same thing with the one I built.

Figure 1 shows the final product. It was built of native spruce and pine obtained from a local sawmill, spruce poles from the woods, derelict white cedar planks, and one new flotation log, as well as a number of bits and pieces of old flotation, which were obtained at no cost. The galvanized fastenings were probably the most expensive items. The

1

Figure 1. The new float.

total cost of the float was around a hundred dollars. When the tide is in, there is about nine feet of water off the float, which allows me to lie there from half-tide to half-tide, and that's long enough to do a lot of work. The float is quite suitable for loading and unloading gear at the start and finish of the season, for allowing people to board or disembark, and for dock sailing.

This chapter describes the construction of the float; a later chapter will explain how it is converted into a motorized barge for setting and lifting a 400-pound mooring.

Before beginning construction, it always pays to let the word out that a project is in the works. In my case, doing this resulted in a lot of free chunks of flotation, as well as the information that a derelict float had been washed up on a friend's waterfront. It was decked with two-inch white cedar planks six feet long. I concluded that six feet would be just the right width for my float. It's 12 feet long.

Figure 2. The float under construction.

Figure 2 shows the float a-building. The four main timbers are 2" x 1" x 12' pine planks. There are two gaps, one in the center and one at the forward end. The center gap became a storage well for lobsters and clams, while the forward one allows you to haul a mooring. During regular use, the forward space is planked over, as described later.

For flotation there is one Styrofoam log, 10" x 20" x 9', plus one chunk of flotation in the center section and a lot of smaller pieces. These are vertical pieces hand-sawed from various-size sections of donated logs. Since they rest on the bottom skids, which are bowed, they had to be sawed in slightly different lengths so that when set in place, their upper surfaces were about level. The sawing was quick and easy.

In Figure 2, two of the deck planks have been spiked on.

Before all the flotation was finally put in place, some hardware items had to be installed. Two half-inch galvanized shoulder eyebolts were fastened through the forward ends. A heavy galvanized ring plate for lifting and hauling was screwed on the end of the center section. Two vertical 2" x 5" "side boys" were through-bolted with half-inch galvanized bolts. These side boys hook the float to the catwalk and are high enough to grab when you lose your balance.

Figure 3 shows the float finished and in the water. The forward opening (beneath the dinghy) is decked over, and it has a facing piece with a washing-machine roller on its upper edge for dinghy handling. There is a trap door over the lobster well, and two wooden stanchions connected by a short rail. A boathook and an oar are clipped on at one end, while a davit and winch are pivoted at the other. The davit is put in place only when you want to lift the end of the catwalk to free the float.

Figure 3. The float in the water with the catwalk in position.

Figure 4 shows construction details for the basic frame of the float. As mentioned earlier, the four longitudinals, as well as the six-footer at the after end, are pine planks from the lumber mill. They are full-dimension 2 x 10s. Except for one 2 x 8 skid, the rest of the stuff came from my scrap pile. When I ran out of stock, I headed for the moanin' bench. About that time, my good friend Dick Feyler showed up and bailed me out. He said he had a spare 2 x 8. We drank to that.

The corner 4 x 4s happened to be oak and hard yellow pine. Since the overall width is six feet, each of the open spaces is a little more than 21 inches wide, and that's just right for the width of the flotation pieces. I used ⅜-inch galvanized carriage bolts and washers at the corners. It took 30 that were 6½ inches long, and two 8½-inchers. These two longer bolts go through the inner 2 x 10s, the 4 x 4, and the end of the six-foot 2 x 5 that is fastened on horizontally outboard of everything else. This 2 x 5 becomes a timber for lifting the boat, as well as the base for a motor bracket. The well in the center for the lobsters was bulkheaded off with one-inch boards fastened to two-inch corner posts. It has a bottom of 1" x 1" slats nailed to the cross tie.

After the pieces were sawed to length, I leveled up a couple of timbers for a building platform. The various components were clamped together one after the other, and bolt holes were drilled. At this stage, the frame was upside down so that I could spike on the cross tie and skids when the time came. After all the holes were drilled, the clamps were removed and all surfaces and holes were soaked with pentachlorophenol, or "penta." It's true that salt water is a good preservative, but you still get undiluted rain, especially after the float has been hauled up on the bank.

Next, the frame was assembled again and bolted together. After making sure it was square, I spiked on the cross tie and the three skids. The cross tie at the center of the float goes on first, causing the skids to bow down over it when they are added. (This is the reason for sawing the flotation pieces in different lengths, as mentioned earlier.)

The bowed skids make it easy to launch the finished float down a steep bank. When the float is hauled out, the skids are slimy, so it comes up the bank without much fuss.

In Figure 5 the basic float is finished: the two-inch cedar decking, the rail and stanchions, the outboard bracket, the trap door, the side boys, and the cleats alongside the forward opening to support the short deck pieces that go there. There are two eye-straps (one on each after corner) that hold steering pulleys when the motor is rigged to make the float into a barge. The two hinges and three half-hinges are galvanized and have brass pins. The three half-hinges anchor the feet of a lifting tripod that is installed when it is time to handle the mooring. (More about that later.) There are three cleats on deck (two forward and one aft) and two heavy staples driven into the face of the float to anchor the face piece/fender board (Figure 6). The staples are in addition to the two galvanized eyebolts mentioned earlier.

The face piece/fender board shown in Figure 6 also serves to keep the short decking pieces from sliding overboard. The spikes in the cut-outs at the bottom of the fender board drop into the eyebolts; the slots near the top slide over the heavy staples, and spikes drop down in oversize holes drilled in the face board, and through the staples, thereby securing the fender board.

The face piece goes on and comes off very easily, and it stays put when you want it to. The wringer roller is very handy for hauling the pram up on the float and for shoving it off. While I'm sure that hardwood blocks would be all right for the bearings, I happened to have a pair of galvanized awning fittings that did the trick. I had to cover them with plastic piping to keep the dinghy from getting scratched when it sometimes slid sideways, ran off the roller, and caught on the roller supports.

For a fender along the front of the float where the boat ties up, I stuffed old tennis balls into a section of old fire hose. (All you need is a friend at the fire station and another one with a tennis racket.) It's a tight fit — I had to use a hoe handle to push the balls in the hose. With the balls spaced

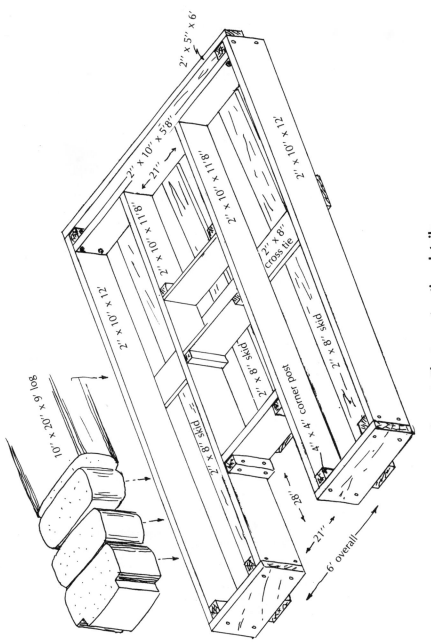

Figure 4. Float construction details.

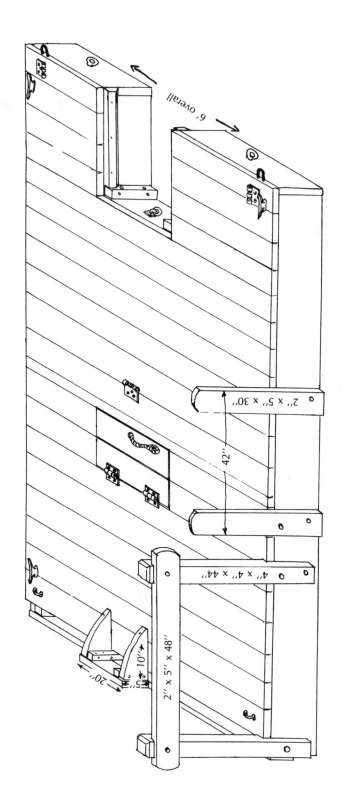

Figure 5. The deck of the float.

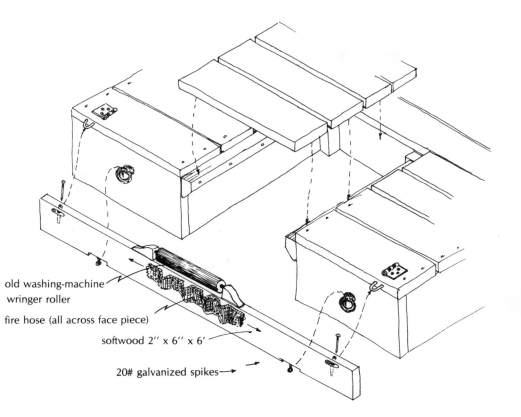

old washing-machine
wringer roller

fire hose (all across face piece)

softwood 2″ x 6″ x 6′

20# galvanized spikes→

Figure 6. The face piece for the float.

every six or seven inches, the in-between parts of the hose can be fastened to the float with galvanized nails.

During the entire planning and construction of the float, I kept wondering what would happen when I had a 300-pound mushroom and 150 pounds of chain hung up in the cut-out at the front of the float. Afloat, awash, or submerged? Well, I've pulled the float under a time or two when we were down in mud, but after I get most of the chain and myself moved aft, she always comes up with the goods.

2

Eyebolts and the Catwalk

Before starting to build the float, I had to find a suitable waterfront location for it — with a place on shore where the catwalk could be anchored. The ledge at the shore had to be dry at high water, had to be broad enough to take two eyebolts spaced at least six feet apart and level with each other, and had to drop off abruptly into deep water so that only a moderate-length catwalk would be necessary.

I found that we had a place that satisfied all the requirements. At low tide the float would rest on a level area of seaweed-covered flat rocks with a clam flat beyond. At high tide there would be about nine feet of water off its face. There were two large rocks just off a ways, but the boat would clear one of them and I took a good bearing on the other. There would be room to sail in to the float without getting too close to the rest of the shore-front ledges, and the location usually was well protected.

On other occasions we had used eyebolts leaded into holes

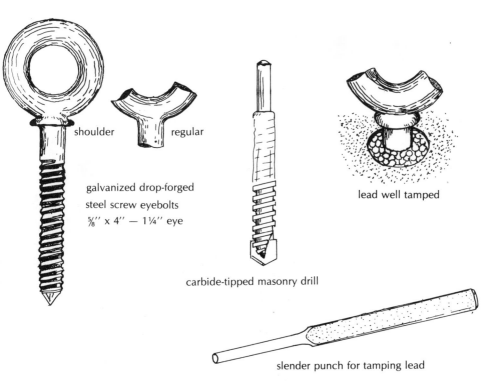

shoulder   regular

galvanized drop-forged
steel screw eyebolts
⅝″ x 4″ — 1¼″ eye

lead well tamped

carbide-tipped masonry drill

slender punch for tamping lead

Figure 7. Eyebolts and their installation.

in a ledge, and, since the system worked well, I planned to anchor my catwalk the same way. The width of the ledge determined the distance between eyebolts, so I set them first and then built that end of the catwalk to fit.

In Figure 7 is a ⅝-inch galvanized eyebolt. For this job the eyebolts must be drop-forged, not cast, since the latter are too brittle. They would snap off as soon as winter ice slammed into them. Eyebolts come in regular and shoulder styles. The regular type is a little more convenient to install, but the shoulder type is easier to find and works all right if the hole is not too deep. The shoulder needs to be at least a half-inch up from the surface of the rock so that you can tamp the lead after it has been poured into the hole.

To make the holes I used three sizes of carbide-tipped

masonry drills up to an inch in diameter. (These can be sharpened on a "greenstone," vitrified green silicon carbide, in a grinder.) After marking the spot where we hoped to drill, I shaved down a two-foot 2 x 4 so it would slide through the handle of a half-inch drill, put in my smallest carbide bit, and called my wife. Bracing ourselves so we wouldn't rock around and snap the bit, we sat at either end of the 2 x 4 and began the slow drilling process. Occasionally the bit hit a softer layer and the work was easier.

When the hole was as deep as we wanted it, we changed to the next-size bit and enlarged the diameter of the hole. This went faster. Finally we drilled it out with the one-inch bit. This drilling was done without adding water to the hole. After we drilled the second hole, I took down a bicycle pump, stuck the hose in the holes, and blew out the dust. Then I plugged each one with a cork to keep out any water. (If you're lucky enough to be able to borrow a diamond drill, this task will be much less time-consuming.)

Next it was time to lead-in the eyebolts. A rusty old "plumber's furnace" I had saved for about 30 years was ideal for melting a ladle of lead. After heating the lead, the threaded end of the eyebolt was lowered into the molten lead to get it good and hot. Then I used pliers to place the bolt in its hole, centered and facing the right direction. A couple of pieces of brick held it in place.

Then I carefully poured in the molten lead, slightly more than filling the hole. (This is the time when it is most important that the hole be dry. Any moisture in there would turn to steam, creating a dangerous geyser of hot lead aimed toward your face.) Soon the lead cools and shrinks, and the eyebolt is loose. The final treatment is to tamp the lead thoroughly using a punch and a hammer. This tightens up everything, and the eyebolts will stay put for years.

A measuring tape run from the eyebolt to where the float would lay indicated that we would need a 28-foot catwalk. I hunted up my good neighbor who had some slender, straight spruce in his woods, and he said I could have a couple of them. After being cut and peeled, these measured

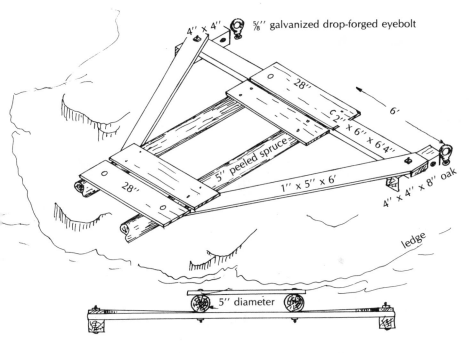

Figure 8. The shore end of the catwalk.

five inches in diameter at the butt and about 2¾ inches at the other end. A drawknife worked best for peeling, and a World War I bolo knife was great for the knots. When the poles were fairly dry, I brushed penta on them.

Figure 8 shows the construction details of the head of the catwalk. I made another trip to the sawmill to get enough rough-cut spruce for the planking. The pieces are a full inch thick, six to eight inches wide, and 28 inches long. They were fastened to the poles with eightpenny galvanized nails. Six ⅜-inch galvanized bolts were used: two through the forward ends of the braces, spruce poles, and deck; two at the base through the 2 x 6, the butt of the pole, and the decking; and two (one each) through the oak block, the outer end of the 2 x 6, and the end of the brace. You might think that the oak blocks would twist around and cause trouble, but they don't. I lash the blocks to the eyebolts with as many turns of

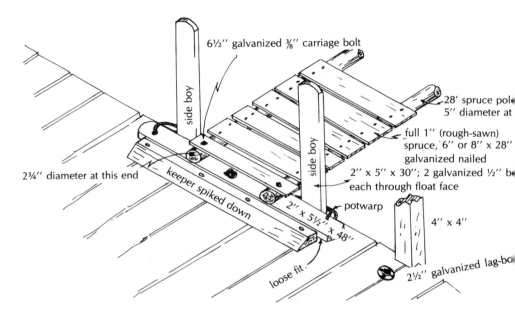

Figure 9. The float end of the catwalk.

potwarp (hard-laid $\frac{5}{16}$-inch synthetic line) as I can force through the one-inch hole in the wood.

Figure 9 shows the outer end of the catwalk and the manner in which it is hooked over the side boys. As the catwalk is being lowered, the potwarp loop keeps the float from drifting until the catwalk is in position with its crosspiece settled in behind the keeper.

I don't know why I made the side boys so tall, but I'm glad I did. You can toss a clove hitch over one when the cleats are full, and they are handy for grabbing to steady yourself before starting the trip up the springy and slightly listing catwalk. (It lists a bit because one of the poles is a little thinner than the other.)

Not having done any stress analyses, I wondered how much this catwalk would take, so initially I suggested that only one person use it at a time. However, before I could mention this to one of our guests, he followed his wife ashore, steadying her as she went. I was relieved that nothing gave way, and someday I'll thank him for making the first test.

The end of the catwalk is too heavy to lift when you want to free the float, so a hoisting device had to be rigged. The hoist used had been made up originally to swing the dinghy out over the bulkhead at our slip during our freshwater boating days. To make it took some hunting around in the old ditty box, and to talk about that I guess I'll have to backtrack a bit.

In 1947 I purchased a 1929 30-foot Gar Wood speedboat that at one time had been used as a rumrunner on Lake Erie. During its reconditioning I took out a bronze floor flange and a bronze bracket from the after cockpit. (I imagine they had been used for daviting shipments aboard.) These pieces became the mounts for my davit, which consists of a bent pipe that has another smaller pipe stuffed up inside for additional stiffness.

Now for the davit winch. First, more history. A student in my aeronautics class back during the war told the group about some government surplus material that he had found. It was cheap, and we all loaded up. I wound up with two hand-crank bomb winches, a couple of flap-actuator motors, a few airplane compasses, a gas tank booster-pump, and an electric feathering propeller motor. The gas booster made an elegant spark-proof bilge pump for the Gar Wood, one bomb winch went on the davit, and the other now hoists and lowers the centerboard in our yawl. I'll admit that I haven't yet found a use for the flap-actuators — nor for the prop motor.

When needed, the davit is rigged easily. (This is covered in more detail in Chapter 4.) It goes through the bracket near the top of the 4 x 4 stanchion on the float and screws into the floor flange. The bomb winch is fixed to a bracket welded to the pipe, and its cable passes through a block at the davit's tip and hangs down near the ring-plate centered at the end of the catwalk. A short pendant having a loop and a float at the top and a hook at the bottom is snapped into the ring and hooked to the winch cable. When the cat-walk is lowered into the water, the end sinks, but when hooking-up time comes, the floating pendant can be snagged with a boathook and fastened to the winch cable. From there on, it's a breeze. A preventer line from the end of the davit tied to part of the float keeps the davit from swinging around outboard.

If you need a float and have only a dirt bank for anchoring the catwalk, you could dig a couple of pits with a post-hole digger and set in two stout posts with the dirt well tamped in around them. A heavy plank on the ground between the posts and anchored to them with eyebolts would support the head of the catwalk. Or you could dig a couple of square pits, fill them with concrete, and set in the eyebolts where convenient. If a float is to lie alongside a wharf, it can be secured with cross chains or with a pair of metal straps bent into U-shaped fittings that can ride up and down two pilings.

The best advice I can offer is to suggest that you look at such installations in your area and get ideas that seem most suited to your situation.

3

Docks and Docking Arrangements

DOCKS AND WHARVES

Out on the Great Lakes you pay overnight dockage or you tie up to a club's guest dock. On the coast of Maine you pay wharfage. Strictly speaking, dockage pays for the water space a boat occupies, while wharfage pays for that part of the structure that a boat takes up at the wharf. What we on the Great Lakes called "docks" should, I suppose have been called "piers," although I never heard of anyone paying "pierage." We used to have slip partners — two boats lying side by side — and dock partners — the boat on the other side of your dock (pier). (Look up the word "dock" in Webster's; I found the original meaning to be quite interesting.)

DOCK BUILDING — THE HARD WAY

There was a time when my brother and I owned a fine old 30-foot gaff-rigger that had been built years earlier in Friendship, Maine. (She wasn't, however, a Friendship sloop.) *White Cap* was located on Lake Ontario, and during World War II it became necessary to move her to my home port on Lake Erie. My cousin and I accomplished this transfer during wartime gas rationing via the locks in the Welland Canal. It was a first-time experience that neither of us ever forgot.

Later that season, I had to come up with a cradle for *White Cap,* so we began to cast about for secondhand timbers. An old wooden barge that had sunk in the river and become a hazard to navigation had been hauled out in pieces; it was being broken up and the timbers were for sale. For about $13 I purchased two 10 x 12s or 12 x 14s that I suppose were 16 feet long. These, together with some used railroad ties and a few 4 x 4s, made a fine cradle.

After *White Cap* moved on to her next loving owner, and I went into the speedboat business with the 30-foot 1929 Gar Wood, those same timbers formed part of the pier that I used in that venture. Figures 10, 11, and 12 will serve to illustrate the construction procedures used in that project.

In Figure 10, the timbers, which were very heavy because they were full of old bolts and burned-off iron drift pins, have been bolted together underneath, floated out on two oil drums (which were later removed), and anchored on shore to prevent them from capsizing (which they would do if given half a chance). The 4 x 4 piles were driven in. Tackles were run from the piles to the timbers to draw the timbers level, and then a supporting crosspiece was spiked home. A makeshift deck was formed by two planks nailed together at their far end, spiked to the outer ends of the timbers, and supported by a line run from the joined end back over a piling to a tackle.

In Figure 11, the intrepid builder atop a step ladder placed on these swaying and trembling planks is attempting to sink a 4 x 4 with a maul.

Figure 10. Splicing a post for the dock.

Figure 11. Dockbuilding the hard way.

Figure 12. The next afternoon — ready for business.

Finally, Figure 12: Ready for customers. There's no deny-ing it — this was not the easiest way to build a dock.

Our club in Ohio was located on the bank of an active river, and each fall we had to remove our docks — and then put them back the following spring. Figure 13 makes it ob-vious why we had to make the effort. Over the years, the designs of the docks, as well as the methods of handling them, underwent considerable evolution. Some of the plat-forms were made of steel, some were covered with sheets of plywood, but the typical platform consisted of 2 x 10 side stringers and end pieces covered with 2 x 6 decking spaced with ½-inch gaps. The docks were all 36 inches wide, as I remember, and from 30 to 50 feet long (Figure 14). The one I occupied had to be more than 20 years old. Every three or four years in the fall, when the dock was out on the bank, we'd turn it over and paint creosote on everything but the walking surface. (If you creosoted the walking surface, you'd track all that stuff aboard your boat.)

Figure 13. On the Great Lakes, winter ice poses a threat to every dock.

To install the dock, the fellows rigged a floating barge with a chain hoist on a boom, an air compressor, and an air hammer/pile driver. With a Jeep to lift the shore end of the dock platform, and with two guy lines on the barge, they could move out, set two 4 x 4s, spike on the crosspiece, move out to the next two 4 x 4s, and so on. The last pair of piles was stiffened with a diagonal brace.

An early experience taught us to leave these 4 x 4 piles fairly tall: One year, during a seiche in the lake, the water in the river rose and then fell rapidly, leaving a boat hung up on a pile with a portion of its forward deck lifted off.

We angled the docks downstream a bit from shore, so that, during a spring freshet, the brush and other junk brought down by high water would tend to move along past the boats rather than pile up against them (Figure 14).

For driving 4 x 4s, we had a hand-held pile driver made up of a three-foot length of 6-inch well casing with a heavy plate welded on top and a pipe handle on either side. With this thing, two fellows working in unison could really do business.

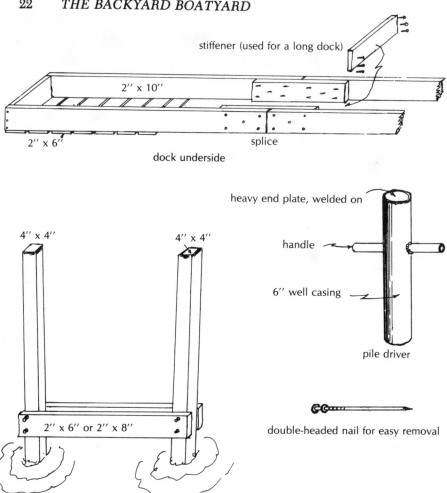

stiffener (used for a long dock)

2'' x 10''

2'' x 6''

splice

dock underside

heavy end plate, welded on

handle

6'' well casing

pile driver

4'' x 4''

4'' x 4''

2'' x 6'' or 2'' x 8''

double-headed nail for easy removal

Figure 14. Dock construction, pile driver.

Another way of setting pilings in soft bottom is by using hydraulics. First attach a water hose and nozzle to the lower end of the pile in such a way that the hose will come loose when you want it to, perhaps with a tricky tie that will let go when you pull on the end of the line. Lower the pile to the bottom, holding it vertically, and turn on the water. The water jet, aimed straight down, blasts a pit in the bottom, and down goes the hose, together with the pile. When the pile is down a couple of feet or more, turn off the water, free the hose, and pull it up. Mud will soon settle in around the pile. Warning: I've never done this myself, but I've heard the process described, and by all accounts, it works.

Sometimes the water level lowers during a dry season, and you find yourself close to the mud at the bottom of your slip. In such a circumstance, we used to tie the boat securely, start her up, put her in forward gear, and let her churn for 15 or 20 minutes. It's amazing what a large hole can be dug this way, although there are a couple of disadvantages. You stand to have quite a bit of silt going through the raw-water pump, and a portion of the tailings will wash over next door and tend to fill up your neighbor's slip. So use this technique only if absolutely necessary, and watch out for the consequences.

In some places, rock-filled wooden cribs are laid up to support a wharf. I haven't built one of these, but I do have a couple of cautionary notes to inject: You'll probably need to get a permit to install one — from the U.S. Army Corps of Engineers, from your state's Department of Natural Resources, or from both. In all probability you won't be allowed to fill the crib with rocks picked up alongshore — you'll have to supply your own. Finally, build the crib plenty high so that a storm tide won't float the wharf away.

A SIMPLE BULKHEAD AND DOCK

Suppose you have a spot along the bank of a lake, pond, or gentle river that won't rip and snort during spring run-off. You've been out in the boat, sounding, and have found a place where the bottom doesn't drop off too fast but will give you enough depth for the boat alongside a modest dock.

The first project is to lay in a supply of timbers: some old railroad ties, telephone poles, or something similar. You'll need a number of 4 x 4s, some 2 x 6s, and some good 2 x 10s each 10 or 12 feet long. If anyone is giving away any old fire hose, get it.

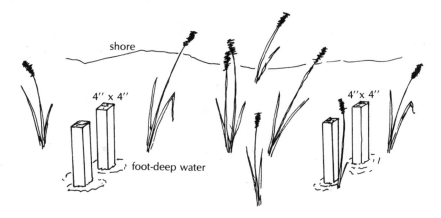

Figure 15. Setting pilings for the bulkhead.

Bulkhead

Take six or eight 4- or 5-foot 4 x 4s, and chop one end of each to a point. Then you and your helper (dock partner?) put on boots and wade out among the cattails to where the water is a foot deep. (If you tramp down cattails, they will help to keep you from sinking down into the muck.) With a maul, drive pairs of 4 x 4s in a line where you want the bulkhead to be (Figure 15). The gap between each pair of 4 x 4s should be slightly greater than the width of your bulkhead timber.

Next, float out the timbers and drop them in between the pairs of 4 x 4s (Figure 16). The first string will quit floating when you drop the next set on top of them. In water that doesn't rise and fall much, I think a bulkhead extending a foot above the water would be fine.

Next, arrange for a few loads of fill to be dropped behind your new bulkhead. (You'll probably need to get a permit for this procedure.) The fill probably won't arrive for a few days, but that's just as well — that will give the bulkhead time to settle in. You don't want to tip it over with a carelessly dumped load.

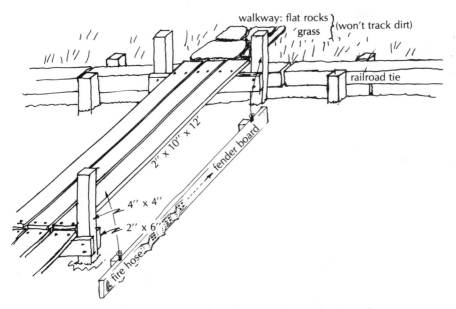

Figure 16. The finished dock and fender board.

Making the Dock

Point a pair of 4 x 4s and drive them down the face of the bulkhead spaced about 30 inches apart, then spike on a 2 x 6 crosspiece having its upper edge parallel to the water and about even with the top of the bulkhead so the decking planks can come and go a bit.

Next you run in with the boat, drop a stern anchor, take the bow line ashore, and position the boat (a pole jammed into the mud might help hold her) so that you can drive the next pair of 4 x 4s from her deck. This pair should be 10 or 12 feet from the first set, depending on the length of your planks. Spike on two crosspieces parallel to the water and the same height as the first one. Float out three planks and spike them in position.

Move out another 10 or 12 feet and repeat the process, trying to make sure that the dock will be straight. Your dock is finished. It may shake and sway a bit at first, but it will firm up as the pilings take a set in the mud. If you think the spans are too springy, set a pair of intermediate piles and spike on a crosspiece.

Leave the dock piles high enough to let you toss a dockline over them conveniently, but saw the piles at the bulkhead flush to prevent them from becoming a hidden hazard as the weeds grow up around them. Nail pieces of fire hose or some other protective material over the rough ends of those 2 x 6s.

Once, when I had a dock like this, I made a fender board out of a light 2 x 6 that was long enough to span the distance between uprights plus a foot more. A block of wood spiked on the inside near each end prevented the board from sliding past a pile and slipping beneath the dock. I nailed old fire hose in a scalloped pattern across the face of the board. To do this, start at one end of the board and nail down the end of the hose with four 1½-inch roofing nails, stick a hammer handle under the hose, drive in four nails past that, pull out the hammer, and repeat the process until the hose is attached all along the board. Two eyebolts, placed in the 2 x 6 as shown in Figure 16, allowed the board to be suspended from two 4 x 4s in the position where it would do the most good, absorbing the impact of careless landings and keeping the topsides away from rusty nail heads. The fender board lasted for years.

After your fill has come and you have graded it back up from the bulkhead, plant grass and make a walk out of flat stones to prevent dirt from being tracked aboard.

If you leave the dock in over the winter, you may come back in the spring and find it boosted up at a jaunty angle from ice working on it. You should be able to drive it back down fairly easily. If, however, your dock is located where there is a spring break-up (as was shown in Figure 13), and great blocks of ice come spinning down-current, it will surely be lost.

A MORE RUGGED BULKHEAD

A bulkhead that I built for deeper water and a higher bank lasted for a number of years because the construction was

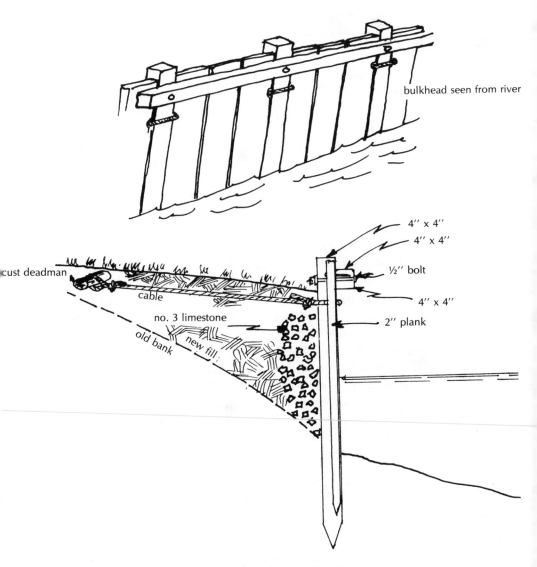

bulkhead seen from river

4'' x 4''
4'' x 4''
½'' bolt
4'' x 4''
2'' plank

cust deadman

cable

no. 3 limestone

old bank   new fill

Figure 17. Bulkhead and bank detail.

more rugged (Figure 17). The 4 x 4s and planks were oak, and all wood was given two coats of creosote and allowed to dry. (Even though creosote will leach out in time, it certainly lengthens the life of a wooden structure.)

Pointed 4 x 4s were driven down in a line, and each was kept as plumb as possible during the driving. The distance between them was a multiple of the width of the planks to be used. A long 4 x 4 was attached horizontally along the face of the piling — clamped, drilled, and fastened near the top of each 4 x 4 with a half-inch through-bolt.

Next, each piece of sheet piling (plank) was beveled to an edge at the bottom, driven home with a maul, then spiked to the horizontal 4 x 4. Holes drilled in these planks on either side of each vertical 4 x 4 allowed a loop of cable to be passed around the 4 x 4, secured by cable clamps, and run back to a deadman that was buried back where the ground was firm (even farther back than shown in the sketch). Small peeled locust logs were used for deadmen, since locust is quite rot-resistant. (A good source of cable is a telephone repairman — I've seen them give it away when they were running new guys on a corner pole.) The tops of the planks were sawn off in a line a little lower than the 4 x 4s.

Experience demonstrated that quite a bit of fill would be lost to the river through the cracks between the planks and knotholes here and there. A second set of planks staggered behind the first would have prevented this but would also have encouraged rot. At that time you could go down the river a little ways with your car and trailer and get a load of crushed limestone for $3 a ton, so this seemed like the better solution. Limestone was shoveled in behind the bulkhead up to water level or a little higher, and then fill was dumped in, graded, and seeded. By the next season, there had been quite a bit of settling, so more crushed limestone was dumped in, followed by additional fill. After a couple of years, everything became stabilized, so all that needed to be done was to mow the grass.

Ten years later these wooden bulkheads were beginning to give trouble — planks rotting out, and so forth. At that time a group of very bright fellows made a deal with a railroad company and obtained the steel end panels from a large number of junked boxcars. Now this portion of the river has an elegant steel bulkhead topped off by a broad channel iron cap. It took a lot of work and ingenuity, but the price was right.

4

The Float Becomes a Barge

Now we're back to the float, that versatile device. Not only can it be attached to the bank by a catwalk (Chapter 2), but it also can be motorized for a mooring-setting or mooring-hauling expedition.

Figure 18 shows the lifting and lowering tripod. It was made with a cedar 4 x 4 that was 7⅓ feet long and two seven-foot 2 x 6s. If the tripod had been much taller, it would be too heavy for carrying around; if shorter, the operator would have bruises on his head from bumping into it.

Each leg of the tripod is supplied with a half-hinge at its foot to engage with the corresponding one of the three half-hinges screwed to the float's deck. The apex is fastened with a 12-inch bolt that should be at least a half-inch in diameter. The bolt passes through a big washer, the slotted hole in a 2 x 6, the first link of a ⅜-inch chain, a snug hole in the 4 x 4, the last link in the chain, the slotted hole in the

Figure 18. The outboard and davit in position on the float.

other 2 x 6, a large washer, and the nut. So it has to be a long bolt. At stowing or carrying times, the nut is backed off, and the slotted holes allow all three legs to be bundled together and tied. When the tripod is in a hauling position, the nut is snugged up to prevent wobble.

The winch (Figure 19) is a free-spooling, heavy-duty model that has a double drive, either 5:1 or 12:1. (Both are used.) It is through-bolted to the 4 x 4 with ⅜-inch machine bolts. As will be described later, this winch is used on two other pieces of equipment.

Two sets of hooks are needed when you are lifting a mooring, but only one is needed when you are setting it. There is a ⅜-inch grab hook for the light chain and a one-inch slip hook for the heavy chain and the mushroom. It's smart to

Figure 19. The float's winch, mooring, and trip-line.

try them for size while the mooring is still on the bank. The holding line is secured to the head of the tripod and supports a similar pair of hooks about waist high; when the hoisting hooks are chockablock, the holding line lets you ease off and take a new purchase. (If a helper is on the handle and the winch is on 12:1, remind him to keep an eye on the hoisting hooks so they don't get swallowed up there — otherwise the line may strain or break.) The block can be any good one, and, depending on the configuration of the hook, you may want to put a shackle on the chain to give it a fair lead.

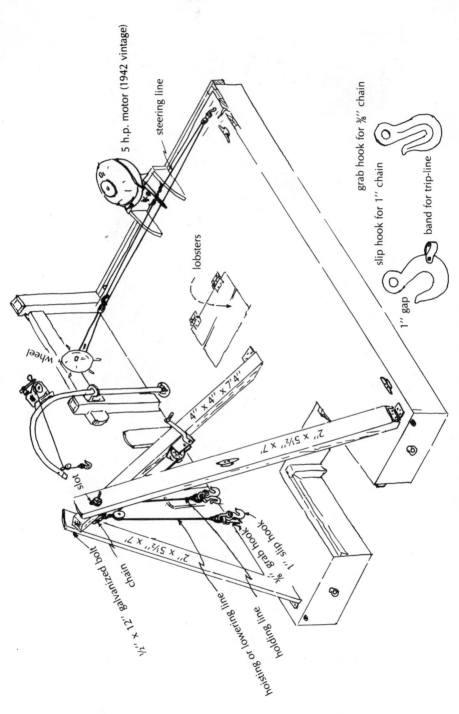

5 h.p. motor (1942 vintage)

steering line

grab hook for ⅜″ chain

slip hook for 1″ chain

band for trip-line

1″ gap

lobsters

wheel

4″ x 4″ x 7′4″

slot

2″ x 5½″ x 7′

2″ x 5½″ x 7′

⅜″ grab hook

1″ slip hook

½″ x 12″ galvanized bolt
chain

hoisting or lowering line

holding line

Figure 20. The float rigged for lifting or lowering.

When you are going to lower a mooring, you need only one hook, and no holding line is needed. The hook is a one-inch slip hook that has been drilled through near the back, where an aluminum loop has been fastened with a slender stainless bolt and nut. A polypropylene trip-line is fastened to this so the hook can be detached when the anchor is on the bottom. The whole float-barge rigged for lifting is shown in Figure 20.

The outboard that motorizes the float-barge is a 5 h.p. model that I believe was manufactured in 1942 (Figure 21). I used it three boats ago and hadn't known for years what it was being saved for. The motor doesn't want to run wide open, but at half-throttle, we develop a "bow wave."

The motor is steered by a wheel and drum, steering line, and a single and double block attached to the eye pads on the "deck." The wheel rotates on a threaded brass tube screwed into a galvanized floor flange on the face of the rail. The steering arrangement all comes off easily. You could

Figure 21. The motorized float carrying a load of crushed mussel shell.

steer with one foot, but it's more fun with the wheel. And anyway, I had the old wheel in my junk box.

When a fellow gets aboard this barge and goes tooling around the cove pushing up a nice bow wave, he feels, I guess, a little like a descendant of Mark Twain. I don't know why I think it's so much fun — maybe because as a kid I had a raft on a pond.

MOORING SETUP

My mooring setup has a 300-pound mushroom, 20 feet of one-inch chain, a swivel, 30 feet of ⅜-inch chain, another swivel, and about 12 feet of ¾-inch nylon served with marlin and protected by a laced-on leather sleeve where it goes over the chock (Figure 22). (For more specifics, see Appendix A.) A mooring buoy (Figure 23 — I'll describe that in a minute) was made out of a plastic cube that large bottles of chemicals are sometimes shipped in.

When it's time to lower the mooring, I use a gin pole to swing it out over the bank and into shallow water. The float is brought around, the mushroom is hooked onto the trip hook, and the chain and buoy are dragged aboard. We then hoist the mushroom off the bottom — or wait for the tide to do it, as the case may be — and then churn out to the mooring spot, previously located with cross bearings and marked with a buoy. This buoy is a great help. Without it you can become pretty busy — watching one bearing, watching the flag your wife is handling on shore to indicate the other bearing, down-cranking the winch, and starting the motor after the wind or current has shifted your position a boat length or three. Also, being a fellow with an active imagination (i.e., timid), I wear a fat life jacket, carry an anchor on the float, and tow the dinghy rigged with its little motor.

After arriving on station, instead of letting everything run with a clash and a clatter, we winch the mushroom down under control. For lowering the heavy chain, there is a double line reeved through a link at what will be the chain's

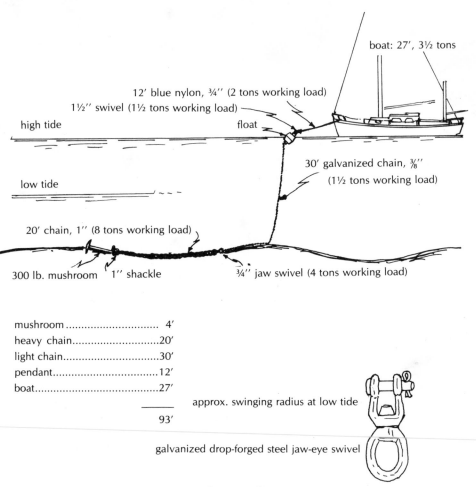

boat: 27', 3½ tons

12' blue nylon, ¾'' (2 tons working load)

1½'' swivel (1½ tons working load)

high tide

float

30' galvanized chain, ⅜''
(1½ tons working load)

low tide

20' chain, 1'' (8 tons working load)

300 lb. mushroom   1'' shackle

¾'' jaw swivel (4 tons working load)

mushroom .... 4'
heavy chain ....20'
light chain ....30'
pendant ....12'
boat ....27'
_____
93'

approx. swinging radius at low tide

galvanized drop-forged steel jaw-eye swivel

Figure 22. The mooring setup.

upper end. One end of the line is made fast and the other
part is cleated on the port tripod leg. It's important to stand
clear, since, at some time during the lowering, the heavy
chain will go crashing overboard until it is brought up short
by this line. As the strain builds up, this line is eased.

When the mushroom hits the bottom and the line from
the winch slacks off a bit, the buoyancy of the polypropylene trip-line will disengage the hook, which can be drawn
up quickly. If not, a slight tug on the trip-line will effect its
release. So far, this has always worked. We then drift down-
current, paying out the chain line until the chain is
stretched along the bottom rather than piled in a heap.
Since the line is double, we can cast off one end and draw it

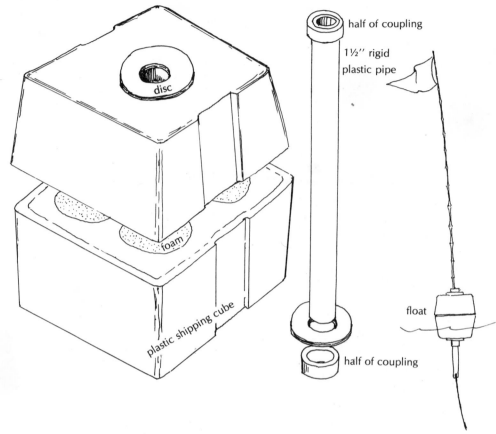

Figure 23. The mooring and racing buoy.

back up through the chain link. The job is finished as we slide the light chain and mooring buoy over the side — if it hasn't already gone over of its own accord. One man can set or lift a mooring with this rig, although it's handy to have a helper aboard — especially when the wind is blowing.

Lifting the mooring takes longer, since you have to haul up, secure to the holding hook, slack off and lower away, get a new purchase down by the water, and then repeat the process until the mooring is up.

Figure 18 shows the float being rigged for mooring work, but the winch, block, and lines are not yet on. Figure 19 shows the mushroom hoisted for moving out. It is supported by the slip hook with its trip-line attached. The two sizes of chain are shown, as well as the double supporting line threaded through the upper end of the one-inch chain.

On the subject of gear for hauling and setting moorings, I should offer some advice if you are hauling for someone else. And if you have your own motorized barge for hauling and setting moorings, you can be sure you'll be called upon for assistance. Last season, for example, I set six different moorings and lifted them out. If your friend has line run to his buoy instead of chain, you'll need an assortment of hooks and short rope to help get a grasp. But it's something less than good fun reaching wrist-deep into the water to try to lift a 300-pound mushroom through 22 feet by trying to throw rolling hitches around a slimy nylon line. Chain makes the chore a whole lot easier.

THE MOORING FLOAT

The small float that supports the mooring chain starts with a four-bottle plastic shipping cube, if one can be obtained from a friend in industry. (Otherwise, you can use two sections of Styrofoam logs.) The cube is about 13 inches on edge, and, when finished, it will support about 75 pounds before going under. (Thirty feet of $\frac{3}{8}$-inch chain will weigh about 50 pounds.)

The first step in making the float is to fill the holes (the ones in which the bottles were shipped) with two-part polyurethane foam. Defender Industries Inc. sells this stuff in $2\frac{1}{2}$-pound (one quart) quantities. (One quart of the foam will make two buoys, if you don't try doing this in a cold, damp cellar.) Stir equal parts of the two components together in a paper cup, then pour the mixture in the hole you want to fill. If everything is working right, the stuff foams up, filling the void, and then it hardens.

After you have filled all the voids in the two halves of the cube, you can slice off the bulging top of the foam with a hacksaw blade. Each cube half has a hole almost all the way down through its center, and this hole has to be drilled out the rest of the way to allow a piece of 1½-inch rigid plastic drainage pipe to pass through. Two five-inch discs of waterproof plywood or scrap fiberglass about ¼ inch thick are sawed out and drilled for a snug fit around the plastic pipe. Next, saw a plastic pipe coupling across and cement one half to the end of the pipe. Thread the pipe through a disc, then cut it off so that the other piece of coupling, when cemented on, will hold all the parts together snugly. I usually run a bead of gutter mastic around the joint at the equator. You have to be careful about using any old kind of cement, since some kinds will dissolve the foam. A ⅜-inch chain will slide up through the pipe, where it can be secured by the shackle or swivel that will be attached to the pendant.

I've also made racing markers out of these cubes. For that, you use a whole coupling at the bottom and cement on another length of pipe, say, a foot long. This pipe is drilled to hold an anchor line, and it is weighted if necessary. A bamboo flagstaff can be stuck down through the pipe from above.

The mooring buoy I'm now using has lasted eight seasons and looks as though it might be good for another one or two.

5

A Gin Pole

After the first season of dragging the dinghy over the bank at our place, I decided I needed a hoist. Luckily, there is a nice, straight spruce tree growing in the right location for use as a spar tree. Beside it, the bank is steep, with a short, vertical-faced ledge below that is covered at high tide, and next to the ledge is a relatively flat bottom of gravel that makes a good landing place.

As Figure 24 shows, the gin pole resembles a boat's gaff. It is 19 feet long and five inches in diameter at the butt. An oak tongue with its half-inch pin fits between the oak jaws (drilled for the pin), which are bolted to the squared-off base of the peeled spruce pole. Half-inch bolts were used, and the jaws were sawed out of two-inch stock. For a topping lift, a quarter-inch cable is shackled at one end to the eye band at the tip of the pole, and at the other end to an eye pad lag-bolted to the spruce tree about 17 feet from the ground.

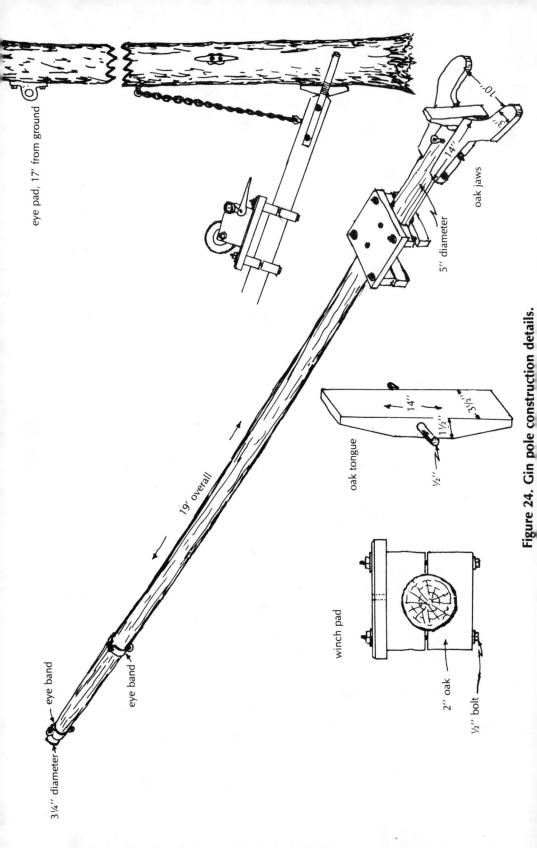

eye pad, 17' from ground

19' overall

eye band

eye band

3¼'' diameter

oak jaws

10''

3''

14''

5'' diameter

oak tongue

14''

1½''

3½''

½''

winch pad

2'' oak

½'' bolt

Figure 24. Gin pole construction details.

In Figure 24 you can see the chain that supports the base of the pole. Each year or so, as the tree's girth increases, I need only hoist the jaws a little and shorten the chain. When the tree gets too large to support the pole at a workable height, the jaws will have to be bandsawed out a bit to give more room.

A pad clamped on the pole holds the winch when there is something heavy to be lifted — such as the mooring, the catwalk, the end of the float, or a heavy timber that has floated in with the tide. For lighter loads, such as the dink, there is a luff tackle hanging from the eye band. I slap on a lot of grease under the tongue and jaws, and, as far as I can tell, this hasn't hurt the tree. The bark has been smoothed and polished, but it is still there. Each season I paint the pole with penta or creosote or deck oil, and it appears to be standing up to the weather all right.

The eyebolt that supports the chain is on the seaward side of the tree, and, even though the spruce does not lean, this feature causes the pole to swing out over the water when it gets a chance, so a one-inch line is looped over the tip to control the swing.

The tree is quite close to the water's edge, and I worried that a heavy load might pull it out by the roots — until the time came when it had a good test. I had winched the 300-pound mushroom up from the bank and hoisted loops of the chain with the tackle, so the pole was supporting about 500 pounds 19 feet out from the tree. As I tossed the light chain over the bank, suddenly the whole load swung out over the water with a great creaking of oak on spruce. I'd forgotten to secure the guy line. I was delighted to see the spruce just sway a little as the load swung back and forth over the water.

Figures 25, 26, and 27 show the launching of the float (which in these photographs still has a padded edge of half-round foam) with the gin pole. In Figure 25, the outboard end has been lifted, and some prying with a 2 x 4 has started it toward the edge of the bank. In Figure 26, the float is farther on its way, and in Figure 27, it is about ready for the

Figure 25. Hoisting the float with the gin pole.

Figure 26. The float poised on the bank.

Figure 27. The float goes down the bank.

water. More slacking off, a good shove, and she'll be floating. (After this procedure, the catwalk gets lifted into place.)

Figures 28, 29, and 30 show the haulout procedure. In the first photograph, the winch line is lifting the bow of the float out of the water and up over the beginning of the bank. A tackle hooked to an eye pad up on a birch tree is ready to start the float up the bank. In Figure 29, an old Speedex tractor with a gipsy on one axle instead of a wheel is chained to a post (or use a handy tree stump). With its 5 h.p. engine, the tractor easily started the float up the bank, and when we changed the gin pole winch line to the after end to help lift, the float was soon up and on its leveling blocks for the winter.

The Speedex is now used only as a winch, having lost out for tractor work to a replacement that has a seat and an electric starter. Figure 30 shows the oak lever that is keyed to one axle to keep it locked; on the other axle is a somewhat improved gipsy. The lever and gipsy were made up by drill-

Figure 28. Preparing to haul out the float.

Figure 29. The old Speedex tractor motor.

Figure 30. The Speedex is now a sturdy winch.

ing one-inch pieces of oak with a hole saw the size of the axle. Then a quarter-inch hole was drilled at the edge of the large hole, squared with a file, and fitted on the axle and its key. When all pieces slid together nicely, they were drilled, fixed with waterproof glue, and bolted together. The pieces were arranged so the grain of the wood ran in opposite directions, lending strength to the whole device.

Two old engine valves that lock the skids to the dolly can be pulled out and the rig can be slid to the ground near the post if it seems advisable. An old one-horse motor is shown supplying the power. It actually did succeed in dragging the float up the bank, but it made such a fuss about it — sputtering, fuming, and stalling — that I later put the five-horse motor back on. This engine runs a couple of other pieces of equipment in addition to the winch.

With the gin pole properly rigged, one man can launch and haul the float and catwalk at the beginning and end of the season — but if you have a willing helper, that will make the whole job just that much easier.

6

Unstepping Your Own Mast

For a number of reasons, I wanted to handle my boat's mast myself, and this called for another examination of the shoreline to see whether there was a suitable place for some kind of gin-pole setup for that. There was.

The same ledge that anchors the catwalk has a weed-covered cleft in its face about the same shape as the boat's bow. At about two-thirds tide, the water is deep enough to nose the boat in close so a person on shore can grab the pulpit while the stern is made fast to the float. (The first few times I brought her in, I hung rope fenders over the edge of the cleft, but we never touched, so these were dispensed with.)

A pocket in the upper surface of the ledge looked as though it might anchor the heel of a pole, and a spruce on the edge of the bank nearby was in fine position to serve as a spar tree. Ideal.

After some sketching and figuring, I decided that a

35-foot pole would be long enough to lift and step the 38-foot mast. The mast would be supported just below the spreaders, but since it had to clear the cabin top, and because I might want to work at full high tide, I figured in a little extra length.

For this project, I took a war-surplus alidade into the woods to measure the height of the tree I wanted. I got all set up, measured the base line, looked up the angle for a 35-foot side opposite, set the alidade, and sighted on a knot well up on the tree. The tree looked usable even above the knot, so I cut it down. Before sawing it off at the knot, I thought I'd better measure just to make sure. Well, did you know that alidades are not calibrated in degrees? I didn't. It was not even close to 35 feet to that knot, but there was enough good, stout wood above it, so luckily I got my full-length pole. I learned a valuable lesson — almost the hard way — but I still haven't gotten around to solving the mystery of the markings on the alidade.

After a session with the drawknife and bolo knife (Figure 31), the tree became a pole tapering down from a five-inch diameter at the butt to a 2½-inch diameter at the tip. Figure 32 shows the construction of the mast-stepping gin pole. I needed an eye band with four eyes, but the only one I could find was 3½ inches in diameter. So some three-foot oak slats fastened along the end of the pole provided the needed girth. About a dozen feet from the tip, I screwed on a ring plate for a second topping lift that would take some of the sag out of the pole, but this later appeared unnecessary. Five feet from the butt, a single ratchet winch is bolted on, and two feet below this are two locust cleats — one on each side. These are for the side guys. There are two more cleats: one is for the downhaul and the other is a spare. The heel of the pole has been rounded so it will pivot more easily in the ledge pocket while being raised and lowered. Each year I varnish the pole with what is left in the bottoms of the cans.

Topping Lift. I screwed a galvanized, drop-forged eyebolt into the spruce tree about 15 feet up and hooked a block to it (Figure 33). The free-spooling winch was fas-

Figure 31. Skinning the mast-stepping gin pole.

tened to the tree trunk at about chest height with two ⅜-inch hanger bolts. These bolts are threaded on each end. Coarse threads on one end go into the wood and machine threads take a nut on the other end. For once, I had wit enough to check to see that the winch handle would clear the tree before I began drilling bolt holes. It became apparent that the bolts would have to be set off-center to provide adequate clearance, and that a wedge-shaped back-up pad would be needed to furnish a flat mounting surface for the winch. Because the tree would continue to grow, I incorporated two removable Masonite filler pieces in the pad. After the winch and pad are removed for the season, I grease the exposed bolts with Vaseline and slip short sections of tubing over them. The winch is wound with ⁷⁄₁₆-inch polypropylene line, and, since the drum will not hold enough to let the pole all the way down, a second topping lift is shackled on. This happens to be one-inch Manila.

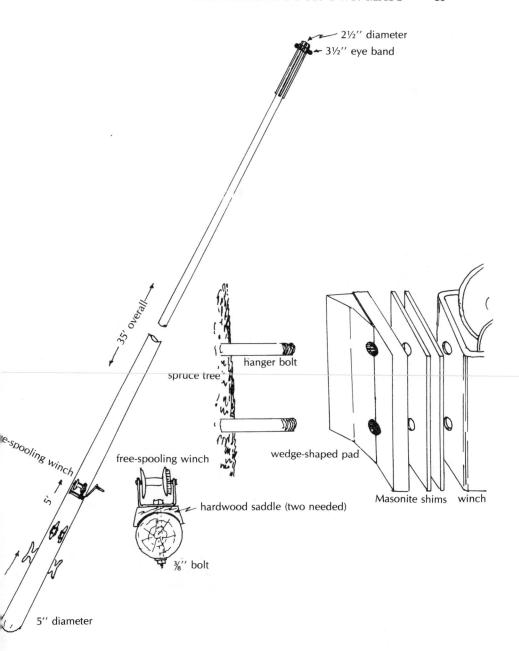

2½″ diameter

3½″ eye band

35′ overall

hanger bolt

spruce tree

e-spooling winch

free-spooling winch

5′

wedge-shaped pad

hardwood saddle (two needed)

Masonite shims   winch

⅜″ bolt

5″ diameter

Figure 32. Details of the mast-stepping gin pole.

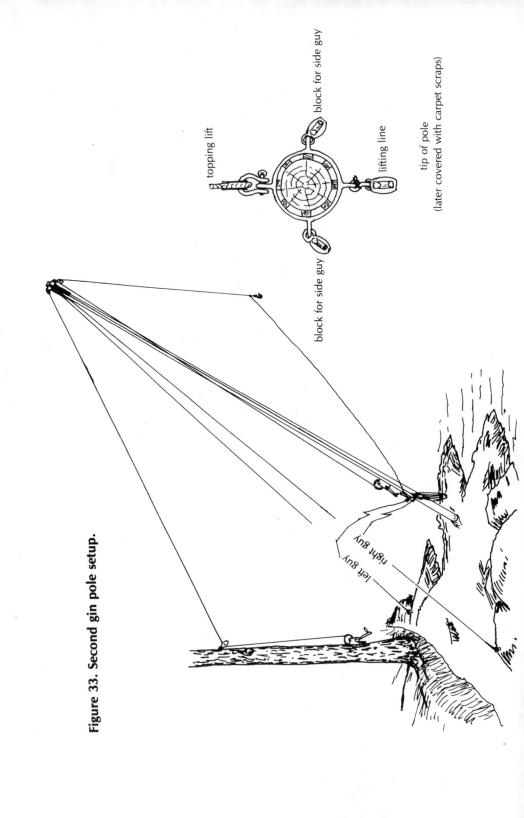

Figure 33. Second gin pole setup.

topping lift

block for side guy

lifting line

tip of pole
(later covered with carpet scraps)

block for side guy

left guy

right guy

Side guys. To make the side guys, I first drilled holes into the ledge and leaded-in ⅝-inch ring bolts — one on either side of the base pocket and about 20 feet away. If these eyebolts could have been in line with, and on a level with, the base of the pole, it would have been very nice indeed — once set, the guys would have needed no adjustment as the pole was raised or lowered. This was not possible here, so the lines have to be tended. It is not really any great chore, since the guys lead through blocks at the pole head and down to the two cleats where they are handled. Each guy is a hundred-foot length of half-inch Manila. (These had been our handling lines while going through locks. They are too long for the current purpose, but I don't feel like cutting them.) The base of the pole is shown in Figure 34.

Raising the mast. After the pole is rigged with its winch, two guys, winch line and downhaul, and topping lift, I tie a crisscross of carpet flaps over the tip to protect the boat's mast in case there is any banging around.

To set the pole in place, it is dragged down the bank until its outer end can be laid across a sawhorse set in the dinghy (Figure 35). While the dinghy floats out, the butt is carried to its pocket and eased into place. When nearly horizontal, the pole has quite a sag to it, but as it is raised, this sag diminishes. Raising the pole and tending the guys requires two people. Some prying with a bar helps to pop the butt down into its pocket.

One note of caution: It is most important that somebody pay attention all the time during raising and lowering of the pole to make sure that the heel does not slip out of its pocket. If it did, someone could be hurt badly.

The first time we had the pole up, I waited until low tide and then hung and jiggled around on the lifting line. Nothing happened, and since the mast weighs 135 pounds and I weigh considerably more than that, I hit the sack that night feeling smug and happy. A wind came up about midnight, and the next morning we found the miserable thing blown over backward in a bunch of alders. So much for smugness! Now, if I have to leave the pole, I crank it down a bit.

Figure 34. The base of the gin pole.

Figure 35. The pole rests on the dink.

Figure 36 shows the pole erected. When the boat is brought in, it is a simple matter to raise or lower the pole or guy it sideways until the hook is directly over the mast hole.

Stepping or unstepping requires three people. The first person handles the bow of the boat by its pulpit, keeping it from touching the ledge and being ready to make minor changes in its position. The second person helps carry the mast and operates the lifting winch. The third person helps carry the mast, pulls or places pins, and guides the mast through its partner and onto or off its step.

For lifting, we use a ¾-inch nylon strop that has an eyesplice in each end. This is passed around the mast, and the ends are secured with a light binding. One end of a downhaul is placed around the base of the two eyesplices, and then the lifting hook is fastened into the eyes and moused. When the strop has been cranked up snug under the spreaders, tension is applied to the downhaul and its bitter end is made fast to a mast winch.

The same arrangement is used when stepping. In Figure 37, the mast is being lifted gradually higher. As that happens, the third person, aboard the boat, will guide the butt aboard and aim it down the mast hole. In Figure 38, the shrouds and stays have been secured and the boat has been brought around to the face of the float.

Figure 39 shows the mast and gin pole on the storage rack where the mast spends its winter and the pole stays most of the time. The rack's posts were set into the ground after being creosoted, then their tops were sawed off level and U-shaped oak crosspieces were spiked on. A line stretched between the posts near the ground acts as an anchor for the winter cover, which has been treated with waterproofing and fitted with brass grommets along each edge. Lately I've hung the pole beneath the supports to allow the cover to shed rain and snow. We clean and wax the mast before storing it.

Figure 40 shows a mast and pole dolly made from a piece of plywood, two old lawn-mower wheels on a steel axle, and a couple of bandsawed blocks lined with carpet. This

Figure 36. The pole is cranked up.

Figure 37. The mast being raised prior to stepping.

Figure 38. The mast in position.

Figure 39. Pole and mast stored for the winter.

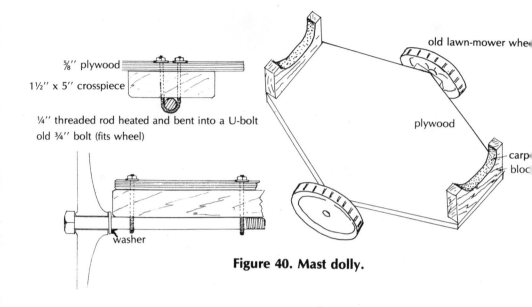

Figure 40. Mast dolly.

works pretty well anywhere that the ground isn't too uneven.

A little more talk about handling masts. Years ago when six or so of us were carrying *White Cap*'s mast, with heavy fittings, an old-timer told me to support it in my hands held a couple of inches above my shoulder rather than on the shoulder itself. Reason: If the others carrying the mast step down over something while you're still on it, momentarily you will be supporting the entire weight of the spar, with a good chance of winding up with a broken bone. You need the shock-absorber effect of the arms-up attitude.

A 38-foot aluminum mast on the ground seems like a reasonable object; it weighs around 140 pounds with its winches and standing and running rigging. However, hanging by a string, or so it seems, up in the air with things rattling and slapping around, it appears to have become a lethal weapon that probably weighs a ton and can come crashing down at any moment. It is best to remember that it has not, in fact, suddenly taken on more weight as well as nefarious and diabolical intentions. Just make sure that your lifting rig is secure, and hook on to the mast somewhere above its balance point. Have confidence.

Some clubs have hoists you can use to step your mast. As my son Jim points out, an extension ladder will work nicely. You need to be able to come in along the face of a wharf. Lag two pieces of 2-inch angle iron to the wharf's deck at a distance from each other slightly greater than the width of the foot of the ladder. To anchor the ladder, slip a rod through holes predrilled in the angle irons and near the bottom of the ladder rails. This assembly can be made up previously at home. Rig two side guys from the head of the ladder to cleats on the wharf as well as a topping lift or backstay straight back to whatever you find to fasten it to. A rope falls hung from the top of the ladder completes the rigging. With the help of a couple of friends, you set up the unextended ladder and take up on the guys and topping lift. The fellow who owns the mast gets to extend the ladder a rung or so at a time, after which the guys and topping lift are readjusted. When you get enough height (remember that you will support the mast a little above its halfway point and that the boat is below the level of the wharf, if it is), haul up the mast, *carefully* adjust the topping lift to center the mast over the boat, lower away, and put in your pins. The whole job should take something over an hour from setting up the ladder to putting it back in your truck.

I knew one fellow who welded up a hook, hung it over the edge of a railroad bridge spanning a river, hooked on a long tackle, ran his boat up under it, hoisted his mast from horses on deck, and stepped it. This never seemed to me to be an easy way, but I guess he thought it was — it didn't cost anything, anyway.

7

Cradles, Trailers, Marine Railways

The new boat owner customarily enters the world of cradles and trailers sometime during the early part of a boating season. Eventually certain chores demand attention, and one of the first jobs is to provide a cradle, unless the boat came equipped with one.

CRADLES

At present prices, if you are able to provide the timbers and build a cradle yourself, you will probably save about $500. A particularly rugged cradle is shown in Figures 41 and 42. It is intended to be dragged out of the water and over rough ground while carrying a 4-ton (plus or minus) boat in it. To be exact, the boat is 27 feet overall, with a beam of 8 feet 7½ inches and a draft of 3 feet. It displaces 7,000 pounds. The timbers used for the cradle are:

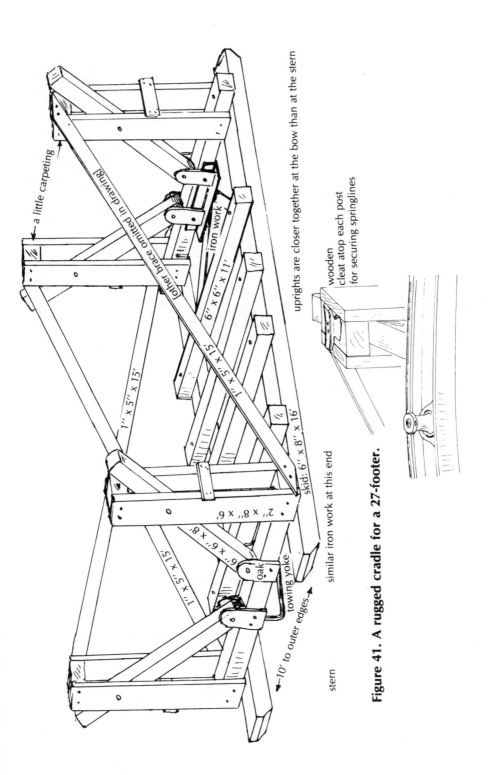

a little carpeting

uprights are closer together at the bow than at the stern

[other brace omitted in drawing]

iron work

6" x 6" x 11'

1" x 5" x 15'

1" x 5" x 15'

skid: 6" x 8" x 16'

2" x 8" x 6'

similar iron work at this end

6" x 6" x 8'

Oak

towing yoke

wooden
cleat atop each post
for securing springlines

stern

◄─10' to outer edges─►

Figure 41. A rugged cradle for a 27-footer.

Figure 42. The rugged cradle for a 27-footer.

2 skids — 6 x 8s 16 feet long, spanning 10 feet to the outer
edges;

6 sleepers — 6 x 6s 11 feet long;

4 pairs uprights — 2 x 8s six feet high, with a 6-inch by
8-inch by 4-inch block atop each pair and a couple of 2
x 4 blocks lower down.

4 shores — 4 x 6s or 6 x 6s eight feet long;

4 braces — 1 x 5s 15 feet long.

Iron work — below the rudder can be seen a one-inch
iron bar bent into a towing yoke and welded to a piece
of three-inch angle iron.

Figure 43 shows the cradle's ½-inch by 3-inch strap iron
braces. Two of these are welded to the three-inch angle iron
and are fastened at the back end by the bolt going through
the number-two sleeper and the skid. The angle iron is
bolted through the first sleeper as well as through the vertical block holding the base of the shore. There is a similar
setup at the other end of the cradle, since the boat is moved
stern-first when launched.

Figure 43. Iron work detail on the cradle.

The fore-and-aft braces are nailed to the uprights and to each other where they cross. In addition to providing rigidity, these braces offer a way of climbing up into the boat.

The block at the top of each pair of uprights is large enough to allow a little extra space for the 4 x 6 or 6 x 6 shores, so they can be adjusted up or down. In the spring, you knock out a wedge, pull a bolt, and lower a shore in order to paint that area of the bottom. Lower only one at a time — the other three will hold the boat.

A well-made and sturdy cradle is a joy to the yard and an economy to the owner; it keeps the boat safe and it cuts hauling-out time. I was able to haul out in 15 or 20 minutes; it took well over an hour to haul out a smaller boat whose flimsy cradle had short, poorly located shores with nothing showing above the water. And that required three or four men and a bulldozer.

TRAILER CRADLES

When a boat is too large to be floated onto a trailer that has been backed down a ramp, there are different requirements. In this case the boat will be lifted out of the water by a crane or TraveLift and lowered gently onto its cradle. The steel trailer frame supplies strength and rigidity, so the cradle can be lighter.

Figures 44 and 45 show the same 27-foot boat as it was first handled on land. Notice that the sleepers rest on the trailer frame and that the skids are bolted on top of them. This was done to ensure that the rig would be low enough to fit under the crane. The pads on top of the shores — as well as the post beneath the forefoot — were carpeted.

This cradle was built of 2 x 6 planks bolted together side by side in groups of three, 4 x 4s for the shores and forefoot post, and 1 x 5s for the bracing. The 2 x 6s were from an old dance hall that was being torn down; they had been laminated to form its framework. I poured on the creosote two or three times, but by the end of nine years, these timbers were full of dry rot.

THE TRAILER

I was told that Inland Seas built this trailer to handle one of their 30-foot Steel Clippers. The specifications are as follows:

Length overall — 20 feet
Span between fenders — 5 feet 7 inches
Tread — 6 feet 8 inches
Frame — 5-inch channel iron
Axle — 1¾-inch square bar stock hung on heavy leaf springs
Tires — 6-ply 8.90 x 15
Brakes — 6-volt Warner electric. A 6-volt battery was carried in a nest in the trailer tongue.
The trailer was most able: the former owner had used it

Figure 44. A lighter cradle for trailering.

Figure 45. The trailer.

to tow a 30-footer from Ohio to Florida. After the rig had sat in the backyard all winter, I had no trouble moving it with a standard-size car using an ordinary hitch. A delicate touch on the electric brake control, which was temporarily attached to the car's steering column, would sure slow us down. I tried towing the boat at 50 m.p.h. and found no problem at all. Since the launching crane was only about six miles from my backyard, I normally kept my speed at about 35 m.p.h.

FOUR-WHEEL NONTANDEM TRAILER

Figure 46 shows the chassis of a heavy 1927 car with a cradle U-bolted to it. The cradle was made of 2 x 10s fore and aft, with bunks sawed out of the same stock to fit the contour of the boat's bottom. The forward bunk was built up with additional wedge-shaped pieces that were braced with triangular pieces and with vertical 4 x 4s bolted on in the corners. A pipe tongue was rigged to steer the front

Figure 46. A 1927 auto chassis under a 30-foot Gar Wood ex-rumrunner.

wheels. This type of steering works well except when you're trying to back up the car, and then it's next to impossible. I bolted a plank to the front bumper of the car and fastened to that a bracket with a trailer ball. This made it easy to back the trailer down the driveway and into the road. A four-wheel *tandem* trailer, of course, handles almost like a two-wheeler.

A CONVERTED HORSE TRAILER

The 20-foot inboard pictured in Figure 47 weighed about a ton. The manufacturer supplied plans for the cradle, and, since the boat was plywood planked, care was taken to see that it was placed on the cradle with the frames directly over the cradle bunks. The trailer was built up out of 3-inch angle iron welded together to make 3-inch box pieces. Since the trailer was intended to transport horses, it had no springs. We extended the tongue, put a strut under it, and bolted the cradle to it with heavy angle-iron brackets.

Figure 47. A 20-footer on a converted horse trailer.

This rig took care of the 20-footer locally for six years, then carried it to Connecticut, later to Maine, and finally back to Connecticut. For a number of years now, this 23-year-old trailer has been transporting my son Jim's 24-foot Ostkust sloop to his Connecticut backyard each fall. The cradle he uses there is welded steel with adjustable shores.

COMMERCIAL MARINE RAILWAYS

Most commercial yards have a car that moves boats out of the water. The car is a heavy affair with lots of iron about it; it won't float. It usually rides on double-flanged wheels on the rails, and, in the case of very large cars for big craft, the wheels will be wide enough to ride on one pair of rails each. Your boat will be moved off the car after it brings her out, and you need to find out just how this moving will be done. If you have a powerboat that will be slid on butter-boards along ways, all you really need is a pair of bunks and a few wedges. For a keelboat, a cradle would be better. If your boat is going to be dragged around the yard by cable or by bulldozer, a stout cradle is necessary. If a TraveLift is to do the job, something pretty simple will suffice. Look around to see what the other boats in the yard are sitting on.

In the railway described here and shown in Figure 48, two skids on the car line up with one pair of ways (parallel and level timbers supported by piling or blocks). Butter-boards are placed on the skids, and then the bunks for the specific boat are placed on the butterboards. The butter-board is an oak plank that has heavy metal pieces at either end extending down to keep the board from slipping off the ways and up to keep the bunk from slipping off the board. A towing eye is welded to each end. When one pair of ways is full, the car is drawn along to the next set.

If the car is on a railway that brings the boat out of the water, the bunks must be chained down. (When the boat is lifted in slings and set down on the car, chaining is unnecessary.) The car has uprights at each corner to aid in

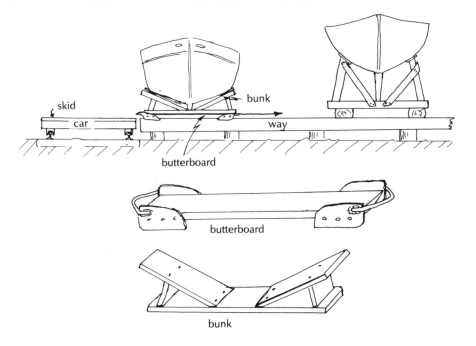

Figure 48. Marine railway with bunks and butterboards.

setting the boat just right. Car and boat ride up and out, and the car is stopped when it lines up with the ways. A chain yoke attaches the two butterboards to a towing cable, which draws the boat off the car and along the greased ways until it arrives at its assigned location. The bow is jacked up, the butterboard is withdrawn from beneath the bunk, the bow is let down, and then the stern is eased down. Finally, the chain is unhooked and the crew is ready for the next boat. When the boat is placed in a cradle, two jacks can be used under the skids until each butterboard is freed.

One principle that every boat owner has to remember in regard to a commercial yard is: First out, last in. It's very expensive to have other boats shuffled around at the beginning of the season if you get impatient.

HOME-BUILT RAILWAY

Figures 49 and 50 show my brother's home-built railway. When shopping around for wood for such a railway, ask the sawyer for something with three characteristics:

strength, lightness, and resistance to rot. Here the section up in the yard consists of 3 x 6s laid on cement pads and other blocks. These are connected to 6 x 6s that run down over the shore ledges to low water, The 6 x 6s are removed each fall. (The whole setup is shown in Figures 51 and 53.)

The keel-centerboarder in Figure 49 is supported on two steel I-beams having welded hangers at their ends. Bolted to these hangers, fore and aft, are wooden 2 x 8s. The 2 x 8s terminate in boxed-in portions containing 6-inch cast iron wheels on stainless steel axles (Figure 52). The after end of the cradle is built up to give the boat a level attitude when on land. Well-braced shores and verticals ensure the stability of the boat.

The inboard/outboard boat in Figure 49 rests on a cradle made entirely of wood (detail in Figure 50). Each skid is made up of a pair of 2 x 8s bolted to separator blocks in the center and at each end. Four-by-four verticals were bolted to the skids, and 4 x 8 oak cross timbers were bolted to the

Figure 49. The home-built railway.

Figure 50. The cradle and rail. The arrow points to the end of one of the stainless shafts supporting a wheel.

4 x 4s. The boat's chines are supported by shores attached to a center plank and the 4 x 8 at their lower ends, as well as to the 4 x 4s near their top. Various other supports and braces were added where necessary.

The arrow in Figure 50 points to the end of one of the one-inch stainless shafts supporting a wheel. The two wheels on this side of the cradle run in a two-inch channel-iron track kept in position by 1 x 2 wooden strips nailed on either side. The wheels opposite run on bare wood — no channel iron.

After being hauled up enough with a come-along to get the winter stop-blocks out of the way, the boats are launched using a one-inch polypropylene line wrapped around a heavy snubbing post set in concrete. They are hauled out by a cable wound around a heavy worm-gear winch driven by an electric motor.

Figure 54 shows the last track section that is left in place over the winter. Its end is bolted to a concrete bulkhead

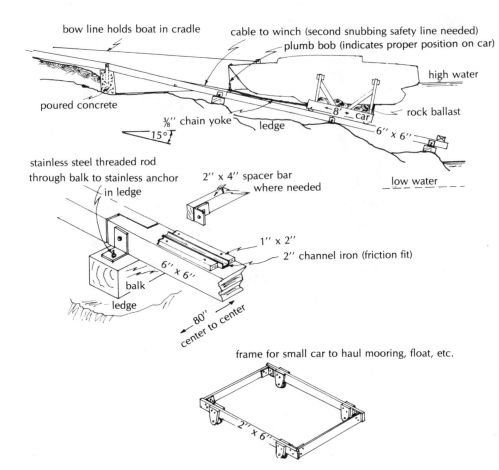

bow line holds boat in cradle

cable to winch (second snubbing safety line needed)

plumb bob (indicates proper position on car)

high water

poured concrete

rock ballast

⅜" chain yoke

ledge

8'

car

15°

6" x 6"

stainless steel threaded rod
through balk to stainless anchor
in ledge

2" x 4" spacer bar
where needed

low water

6" x 6"

balk

ledge

1" x 2"

2" channel iron (friction fit)

80"
center to center

frame for small car to haul mooring, float, etc.

2" x 6"

Figure 51. Haulout on marine railway.

located above the high-tide mark. The track here over the
ledges has a grade of 15 degrees; on the bank it lessens to 7½
degrees.

In the spring, at low water, the 6 x 6s are rollered down,
fastened to each other by lap joints, and bolted to steel
brackets attached to various rocks, blocks, and areas of the
ledges that will allow the opposing rails to be closely
parallel.

During the early days of this railway, my brother's
primary difficulty was in finding a fastening that would
hold the rails and withstand salt water and winter ice. Steel

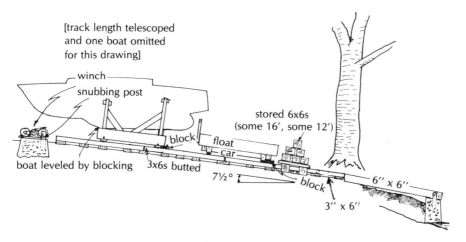

[track length telescoped and one boat omitted for this drawing]

winch

snubbing post

stored 6x6s (some 16', some 12')

block

float car

boat leveled by blocking   3x6s butted

7½°

block

6" × 6"

3" × 6"

Figure 52. Haulout.

cradle timbers are added on as dictated by the shape and attitude of the boat

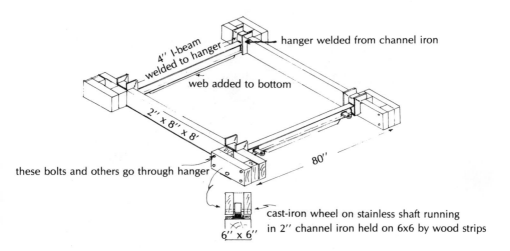

4" I-beam welded to hanger

hanger welded from channel iron

web added to bottom

2" × 8" × 8'

80"

these bolts and others go through hanger

cast-iron wheel on stainless shaft running in 2" channel iron held on 6x6 by wood strips

6" × 6"

Figure 53. The basic marine railway car.

Figure 54. The rail in winter at high tide. (The channel iron has been removed.

Figure 55. The stainless anchor fastening and the punch (second from right).

fittings rusted away rapidly, and poured-cement pads disintegrated quickly. The problem was solved with anchor fasteners set into holes drilled in the rock. Standard ¾-inch-outside-diameter lead-collared anchor fasteners for ⅜-inch bolts were obtained (Figure 55). The threaded steel expansion piece was removed and replaced with a copy machined from stainless steel.

After a ¾-inch hole was drilled in the ledge, the anchor fastener was slipped down in and then the lead was firmly set using a punch and good, hard hammer blows. This punch was machined from ¾-inch stainless steel bar stock. It has a centering lead that slips down into the threaded piece, has a broad circular rim to mash the lead, and is undercut so as not to strike the stainless fitting. Threaded stainless rod can be used rather than bolts, and the fitting at the upper end, wherever it ends, is secured by stainless nuts.

Each spring, when it comes time to bolt on the blocks that hold the rails, or the rails themselves, Sid only has to move a little weed around and locate these fasteners. And there they are — with clean and bright threads, ready for another season.

8

Haulout and Winterizing

It's October, and three days ago our boat was hauled. I had previously used the gin pole to unstep the mast on my boat — along with another one for a friend who owns a sister-ship. After unstepping my mast, I sprayed it with WD-40 (Ed's mast is anodized, so it wasn't sprayed), and then we stored the masts and the gin pole on their three supports, where they are covered for the winter with plastic and canvas.

We get hauled out in a protected cove that has a level bottom, a narrow sand beach where the cradles can be hauled in and out, and a level gravel area on shore where a number of boats can be stored. The people who run this place are most accommodating. If you want them to unstep and store a mast, they will — or they will do the work on the boat and cover it. But if you want to do these things yourself, they don't seem to mind in the least. The spot is about 10 miles from our home mooring.

Our cradles had been rocked down so they wouldn't float and dragged in at low tide to a position where, at about three-quarter tide, we could slide into them. We arrived with the two boats after an hour and a half morning run, and we hit the tide just right. The bulldozer was hooked to the cable running shoreward from my cradle, so my boat went out first. The four posts of the cradle were sticking up out of the water, and, as I eased between them, I felt the keel just kiss a cross member. A couple of minutes earlier would have been too soon. I have painted a stripe on each side of the cradle showing where the sheet winches should line up when the boat is positioned properly. Each post on the cradle has a wooden cleat on top to hold a line used to help keep the boat centered and positioned fore and aft for a few minutes until we are grounded out.

When the boat's weight bears on the cradle, the man in charge of the operation (who is alongside in an outboard) places wedges between the hull and the supporting shores of the cradle where necessary. I leave a supply of these wedges on deck for his selection.

The operator stops hauling when we're at the water's edge, the rocks are lifted off, and we're moved to our spot for the winter.

This entire haulout probably takes 25 minutes, and that's one advantage of having a good cradle (as mentioned in Chapter 7).

By now, Ed's boat was positioned in his cradle. They hooked on and she was ready to come out.

Once in her spot, the boat needed a few more wedges: one oak wedge driven between the forward part of the keel shoe and the stringer under it, a thin wedge between the keel and the last stringer, and a slant-top short post jammed in vertically between the forefoot and the first cradle stringer.

My next immediate chore was to scrub the bottom of the boat before it dried in the wind and sun. For the bottom I use soft copper paint of a type that used to be called "fisher-

Figure 56. The bottom scrubber.

man's red," and at the end of the season there is a good bit of slime on the bottom. The transducer had an 18-inch blond wig of weed hanging from it. I don't paint my transducer, but recently I have seen ads for paint that you can apply safely to one.

In the boatyard where I worked part-time some years ago, we cleaned boat bottoms with water hoses and long-handled brushes dipped in "Mother Nature's cleaner" (any sand on the ground nearby). However, in this case I didn't have the water hose, so I resorted to a bucket of seawater and my home-made bottom scrubber.

My scrubber (Figure 56) is an old long-handled brush with stainless-steel pot scrubbers lashed over its worn-out bristles. I used to use pads of steel wool, but the stainless is far superior. This job is a back-breaker for an old fellow, but it results in a pretty good bottom that doesn't require much sanding in the spring.

Next I go around with a can of WD-40 (or a similar material) with its spray tube in place and shoot a good blast up into each through-hull fitting that has a seacock or a gate valve attached to it. I then operate these valves and cocks until they feel well lubricated.

FLUSHING THE COOLING SYSTEM

The next thing I do since the boat has been used in salt water is flush the cooling system. This engine is freshwater-cooled, so it and its closed system are full of 50/50 water/permanent antifreeze, and that requires only periodic checks. However, the raw-water side, the heat exchanger, the saltwater pump, the exhaust pipe and muffler, and the pipe that takes some of the salt water overboard — all need flushing and, later, draining. I used to place an oil drum on sawhorses beside the hull, fill it with water, and run a hose from it to the through-hull to the engine. Definitely not the easy way! Now I disconnect the lines from the boat's freshwater tank, drain the 25 or 30 gallons into the bilge, disconnect the raw-water intake from the pump, and substitute a length of heater hose that will reach to the full bilge. The idling motor will pump the water out in a very short time. Presto, the two jobs are done at once.

Safety note: I keep this hose and its clamp on board during the sailing season. If for some reason we did take on a lot of water, I could, in about a minute and a half, close the saltwater seacock and substitute its hose at the pump for this one and use the motor to augment the regular bilge pump. An engine will move a lot of water.

DRAINING

Muffler. There is a plug on the underside of the muffler. When it is removed, some water will drain out.

Heat exchanger. There are two plugs — one lets out the antifreeze, the other lets out the raw water. Mine are labeled to avoid a mistake.

Raw-water pump. There is no plug on my raw-water pump. I just back out the machine screws that secure the brass plate at the rear of the pump, pull the plate a little distance from the body of the pump, and it drains. Next I loosen the pulley from the pump and remove the pump belt. I don't want the engine to operate a dry pump when I next start it up. Also, before running it again, I make sure the transmission is in neutral, since, by this time, the packing in the shaft log as well as the rubber shaft bearing has begun to dry out.

The engine. I start the engine and squirt a few shots of motor tune (Casite or a similar product) into the carburetor air horn in hopes that some of it will mist up the inner surfaces of the intake system. Some of it leaks back out. I can't run the engine long because the rubber exhaust pipe is now without its usual cooling water.

Next, the battery can be taken out for basement storage. I remove the spark plugs and squirt in a liberal supply of engine oil from a pump oil can filled for this purpose. The engine is turned over a few times to work this oil around. Since there is a pulley (the one that runs the water pump) in place of a crank, I put the pump belt on this pulley and pull on it to crank the engine. With the plugs out, it turns easily. I then replace the plugs.

I take off the distributor cap and spray it and the distributor with 6-66 or WD-40. I used to replace the cap, but sometimes in the spring I found rust and water in the distributor (perhaps from condensation). Now I cover the distributor body with a cereal bowl or the ship's wash basin, and that seems to work better. I also spray the exterior of the engine.

Gasoline system. I usually try to have the gas tank full at the end of the season, although it doesn't always work out that way. I close the gas-line shutoff, take the plug out of the bottom of the fuel filter (it pays to have a good one), turn on the gas for a short time, and catch in a bowl anything that runs out. This time, there were almost two teaspoonsful of water under the gas. After replacing that plug, I remove the one under the carburetor bowl to drain that dry (sometimes there's a little fine sediment with the gas). Then replug.

I remove, empty, and clean the glass bowl under the fuel pump. If the filter is a good one, the gas in the bowl won't be that dirty, but it's a good idea to take it off now and then anyway; if you don't, the threads holding the bowl fastener may rust and create a problem. (In the spring I drain the filter again and let a little gas run through to catch any water that might have developed over the winter. At that time, I make a very careful check for leaks.)

In the fall, the gas shutoff is always left closed. Every few years I replace the fuel filter element with a new one. One year I covered the engine with a sheet of plastic, and the next spring I found far more rust on it than ever before. I suppose that with temperature changes, condensation dripped off onto the engine. No more plastic.

On the subject of full gas tanks versus empty ones, I had a little 20-foot inboard some years ago with a 30-gallon tank aft. Its filler pipe went nearly to its bottom, as is proper, and the vent pipe to the outside of the hull had a complete loop in it to prevent splash water from getting to the tank. One sunny day that winter I went out to inspect the boat and was horrified to see gas running out of the filler pipe, down the after deck, and over the transom. Obviously the vent wasn't open, the heat of the sun had built up pressure in the tank, and gas was flowing up the filler pipe and out the two notches filed in its edge under the cap. I took off the vent pipe and found a plug of ice in the bottom of the loop where water had gotten in. I put it back with the loop going up and around instead of down and around, and that solved the problem.

While my friend Ed's engine does not yet have freshwater cooling, he flushed it out the same way, the only difference being that he had to get a longer piece of hose to reach the bilge from the water pump near the rear of the engine. He drained the pump the same way (some of them have a plug underneath), took out a plug near the after end of the manifold, removed the plug from the muffler, and opened an engine block drain located back under the alternator.

THE BOAT'S FRESHWATER SYSTEM

The tank has been drained, as described, but it is important to make sure that the water lines are empty and all pumps are dry. My water lines are half-inch copper with unions that can be broken for draining. Some boats have plastic lines that can be manipulated to empty them.

THE HEAD

Every marine sanitation device must be winterized in accordance with the manufacturer's directions. But taking care of a simple old head is only a two-step process. First, dump in a half-cup of a product like Aqualube and pump it around a bit. This keeps the leathers soft and the piston lubricated. After 18 years of this treatment, the head in my craft still works splendidly. Its only repair in that time has been the replacement of a joker valve.

Second, drain the head. There is a plug at the end of the casting, usually under the bowl. To prevent a mess, before I remove this plug I use a battery filler to take out almost all the fluid. The spout will slide easily down past the flap valve at the base of the bowl to get at the water there. I use this same bulb to get the last little bit of water out of the bilge.

SOME HELPFUL HINTS

Before getting to the winter cover, there are a few additional things to remember. I haul the anchor lines out of the chain locker and spread them around on the forward bunks. Since there is a lot of wood even in a fiberglass boat, it pays to open all the storage areas so the air can circulate. Hang up a couple of moth-crystal cakes (paradichlorobenzene) to kill mildew spores.

If you've ever had a cockpit drain plug up with maple buds or dead bees, you'll take my suggestion and put a paper cup upside down over the hole and stamp on it. It works every time.

I used to leave all my tools aboard and the companionway open under the winter cover, but one year recently a prankster made off with my toolbox, so now I take most everything home and lock the boat tight. I have a set of rough hatch covers and companionway boards to put on, so the good ones can be taken home for varnishing.

Finally, the tiller should be lashed so that the wind can't blow the rudder back and forth all winter long.

THE WINTER COVER

It's a simple matter to remove the stanchions and stern rail from the boat, and this simplifies the job of building a cover frame. Mine has an A-frame aft, with a couple of braces going up to the ridgepole (Figure 57). The forward end of this pole rests on a foam pad on the cabintop. Pairs of 2 x 2 frames are attached to a gusset at their top; one is fixed and the other is fastened by a single screw so the assembly can be folded. The gusset fits between two blocks on the underside of the ridgepole. The lower end of each frame, or rafter, is cut on a slant to fit the top of the rail cap, and it has a short

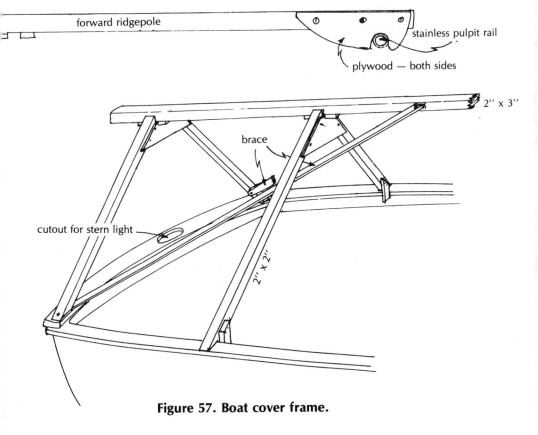

Figure 57. Boat cover frame.

attached leg that fits inside the rail to prevent it from slipping off. I protect the rail with a square of carpet padding at each support point. There are three sets of these frames between the A-frame aft and the back of the cabin. Each one is numbered and marked "port" or "starboard."

The A-frame has a triangular piece of canvas laced to it. When the boat was stored in my own backyard, I had a zipper running up the center of this piece so I could get into the boat easily, or, on hot days in the fall, I could open it up to let the air circulate under the cover. Easy access is no longer a requirement, and the zipper corroded in the salt air, so now the thing is sewn shut. (If you wanted to gain access, however, you could always put in a plastic zipper.)

From the cabin another ridgepole extends forward to the pulpit, to which it is hooked and lashed. There are three pairs of frames for the forward part of the boat, two sets of boards covering the low forward portion of the cabin, and eight short boards along each side of the higher part of the cabin. These rest against the cabin side and are supported on deck just inside the rail. The base of each frame and board is secured from fore-and-aft movement with various lines attached to each in turn and made fast to deck and rail fittings. The tops of the cabin boards are also secured in this manner. Since the cover will rest on the cabintop, hand rails, and companion slide, I throw down an old quilt to prevent chafe.

My boat is fiberglass, but if it were wood, I'd need to make some provision to keep the cover up off the cabintop. A wooden boat must breathe, and dry rot thrives on fresh water, so I'd want more ventilation under the cover — maybe a section of galvanized stovepipe sticking out each end with an elbow pointing downward. Or perhaps some aluminum clothes-dryer pipe. Some covers have weatherproof ventilators sewn into them. I've seen wooden boats with black plastic covers that were fastened by laths tacked around the sheer. Gives me the shrills — I'd think such an arrangement would become a freshwater still on a hot day. Dry rot thrives on warm freshwater-soaked wood.

The final job with the winter cover is to lug up the heavy canvas, unroll it along the ridgepole, flap the sides down, and secure the ties. My cover is dry-waterproofed canvas, and it is very heavy. By the end of the first year, it had shrunk, and it seemed to continue doing so, so I had to have an 18-inch strip sewn along the side. And I have had to use an auxiliary tarp over the bow. Suppliers always say, "Dimensions are cut sizes, not finished sizes," but they don't mention that you need to buy extra to take care of shrinkage as well as hemming.

Some people like to have their tie-downs fairly slack so the wind will blow the cover around and shake off the snow. Others prefer tight lines that keep the cover taut so the snow will slide off. I'm a tight-line man, myself.

I don't know that canvas has any particular advantages as a cover material, but it does last well, and I suspect that it breathes somewhat. However, it *is* heavy, and it *does* shrink. A number of cover materials are listed in the boating catalogs and magazines, but if you are interested in a particular one, ask someone who has tried it. I just received a sample of woven polyethylene. The manufacturer calls it "an oriented, woven, 8 x 8 substrate, high-density polyethylene, coated with 1½ mils of blue poly on both sides." The sample seems to be tough, and it certainly is tight. That's just one of several good materials on the market worth trying.

The last thing to do is to plug the exhaust pipe with a plastic cap or a rubber sink stopper.

HOW LONG DOES IT TAKE?

Here is the record of our boat work in the fall of 1981. It runs from sail drying and removal to final storage of float, gin poles, and all gear. During this time I helped unstep two boats and helped haul one boat besides my own. Two of us hauled four moorings: two of them were dropped on the beach, one was lowered to a car on a marine railway and later moved up the bank, and the other was swung to high ground by gin pole.

Time: 12 days elapsed, 8 days working. Last year it took 16 and 13 days. I'm 72 years old — you can probably work more rapidly.

Here's the day-by-day rundown:

Sept. 24. Brought *Happy Parrot* in, dried sails. Later took off sails, mizzenmast, both booms, and stern rail and stored them in the bosun's locker. Rigged large gin pole (for unstepping masts).

Sept. 26. Moved float, erected gin pole, unstepped two Tartan 27s, lowered gin pole and stored all its gear, and moved float back to its usual position.

Sept. 27. *Happy Parrot* brought to the float. All gear, cushions, etc., removed and stored in bosun's locker. Used SOS and WD-40 on mast, tied it up, and placed it on mast supports.

Sept. 30. *Happy Parrot* motored around eight miles to haulout location. Very cold and wet. Positioning her in the cradle, I fell overboard and got wetter. Hosed and scrubbed bottom.

Oct. 1. Tanks drained, motor flushed and winterized. Afternoon: helped haul Sid's Amphibicon.

Oct. 3. Sid and I hauled the four moorings after I had rigged the float with its motor, tripod, and lifting gear. Unrigged the lifting gear and put it away.

Oct. 4. *Happy Parrot* covered in the morning. Float-hauling gear and equipment set up in the afternoon. Float hauled and blocked up.

Oct. 5. Catwalk hauled and blocked up, small gin pole lowered and stored, and all gear put away. Masts covered with plastic and canvas for the winter.

Work in the spring takes longer because you have to do all that cleaning, painting, and varnishing, but think how much more fun it is!

9

Storage Facilities

Back in the early Sixties, when *Happy Parrot* was a freshwater boat, I sometimes backed her in alongside a shed behind my garage. I could unload gear by stepping onto the shed roof and then through a doorway into the bosun's locker — the upstairs of the garage. Sails, cushions, and other gear, as well as the mizzenmast, both booms, and the spinnaker pole went up there. The spars hung on supports screwed to the rafters. The mainmast was stored down at the boat works.

Later on, when we were clearing our piece of property in Maine, I took a little time off to build a 6-foot by 6-foot tool shed. For some years, the shed stored the bushwhacker, the garbage can, and whatever tools and other stuff we didn't take back to Ohio each fall. After the house was built and the *Parrot* arrived in Maine via the New York Barge Canal and other waterways, the shed began to hold more and more boating gear. However, since the shed was up on a hill near the house, it wasn't too handy.

A couple of years ago, when we knew we were going to be permanent residents in Maine, we moved the shed. I put skids under it, and my friend Bill hooked on with his Land Rover and dragged her down through the berry bushes to a spot under a spruce tree near the water. It is now the boat shed (Figure 58), and it stores all shackles, hooks, rope falls, hand winches, tools, and other gear used in rigging gin poles, getting the float in and out, and so on. Paints, varnishes, brushes, and gas cans for the outboard are also stored there.

We (two sons, two grandsons, and I) built a 19-foot by 22-foot garage (Figure 59) where the shed had stood. Its official name is "Lifeboat Station Number 7," mostly for reasons of whimsey. It also has a bosun's locker. I get a certain amount of flak about not being able to step out of that upper doorway, but I let them laugh. We unload the boat down at the float, pile all the stuff in a trailer, tow it up to the garage with a garden tractor, and then pass, toss, or haul everything up through that second-floor doorway. The mainmast is stored on its three supports, as mentioned in Chapter 8, but the other spars fit up under the rafters.

Any heavy "foreign matter" (such as a snow blower) can be hoisted up to the outside of the doorway with a yard tackle, then hooked to a stay tackle that is secured to the ridgepole inside the garage. As the stay tackle is taken up and the yard tackle is eased off, the load swings in through the doorway, and from there it can be lowered to the floor. Hauling things out and down works equally well.

The first interior view of the garage (Figure 60) shows the moanin' chair, some lines, the old ogee weight clock that gets cranked up once a week, and the ends of the spars in the rafters.

Above the clock is a shelf with a rack beneath it. The rack pivots on two nails at its inner end and is supported by a line that can be slacked off. It stores all of our charts in their portfolio envelopes. When we want to do some winter planning for the next season's cruise, it is easy to select the right envelope from this rack. When we sailed to Maine from

Figure 58. The old boat shed.

Figure 59. Lifeboat Station No. 7.

Figure 60. The bosun's locker.

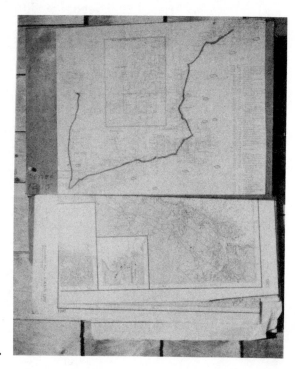

Figure 61. Chart stowage.

Ohio, we had nearly 80 charts on board — a lot to organize and store in a small boat. We sorted them out by series and region, folded each one twice, and placed a reasonable number in each of six envelopes. I pasted a sheet from the chart catalog on each envelope, with the numbers circled to indicate what charts were inside. Luckily, two or three of these envelopes fit in the chart drawer at one time, and the rest could be stowed in a locker beneath a dinette berth. With only two people aboard, it's great to be able to grab the right chart quickly with a minimum of shuffling around.

Figure 62 shows more stowage on the second floor of the garage. On the overflow bed are sleeping bags and life jackets (foul-weather gear is also stored there). To the left of the bed are the sail bags, fenders, and some running rigging. The white cockpit awning is rolled up and stuffed behind a

Figure 62. Sail and gear stowage.

slat between rafters. The boat's cushions are piled on the floor behind the sail bags. Beneath the large fender is an MSD tank.

I like to boast about that fender; it's been through more than 70 canal lockings and also is great when you are rafted up. It's about the size of a duffel bag, the bottom third has had a second layer of canvas stitched on, and the mouth is grommeted so it can be laced shut. I used to fill it with planer shavings, which were springy and certainly cheap. When they got too wet, I dumped them and tramped in a new supply. Now the fender is filled with a combination of plastic kapok-filled envelopes from old boat cushions, pieces of salvaged plastic foam, and foam peanuts that are used for packing. A big advantage of this particular fender is that it doesn't squeak all night. It also stows out of the way in our lazarette.

Figure 63. The dink hoisted to the garage ceiling for the winter.

I have never had trouble with mice or red squirrels in the locker, but I do keep a pretty good watch.

Figure 63 shows the main floor of the garage. The dinghy is hoisted to the overhead with a couple of tackles, and it is secured there with two slings to ensure against an accidental crash onto the hood of the car. Ribbons hang from the skeg to remind me that it doesn't clear my head when the car isn't there. The bow clears easily.

In addition to the anchors hanging on the wall, and a pair of massive galvanized snatch blocks my son gave me, there is a dolly that slips up under the dinghy's bottom past the skeg, and a low horse cut to fit its bottom forward. I usually refurbish the dinghy sometime in April — and she's lasted more than 40 seasons.

It's great fun to be able to store your gear where you can get at it and work on it at your leisure during the winter. Makes the time pass. Even a simple task like shining the brass cabin lamp can be pleasant. Sunshine hitting the 45-degree, dark-colored roof warms up the locker, while down below, if I want to, I can fire up the little woodstove.

10

Fitting Out

It's hard to beat that time of the year when you take the cover off your boat and put away the frame. How did she stand the winter? How much work needs to be done? Time for fitting out.

INTERIOR

I'm always anxious to have the boat come alive in the spring, so after washing down the interior wherever it needs it with Fantastik, I fake the two anchor lines back down in their separate halves of the chain locker and replace the covers for the berth lockers. This restores a little order down below. Then I proceed with my spring checklist.

MOTOR (Freshwater Cooled)

• The drain plug is replaced in the heat exchanger. (See Appendix B for more specifics on engines.) I always brush a little touch of Rectorseal No. 5 (slow-dry, soft-set) pipe compound on all plugs that go into anything connected with water.

• The plug is put back in the bottom of the muffler.

• The back plate of the raw-water pump is tightened up, but the belt and pulley are not yet replaced.

• The top tank is topped off with a 50/50 mixture of water and permanent antifreeze.

• *Distributor.* Wipe out the distributor and spray the body and the cap with WD-40. Examine the points and replace them if they are pitted. I usually have to do this about once every four or five years. Drop a little oil on the felt beneath the rotor. Wipe a little Vaseline on the shaft flats. Squirt several drops of light oil into the oil cup near the bottom of the distributor. Replace the rotor and the cap. (While you're at it, make sure my advice agrees with the manual for your own motor model.)

• *Spark plugs.* Set the gap for your plugs — probably .003, but check your manual. The manual for my Universal Atomic Four calls for the plugs to be torqued in to 30 foot-pounds. I always used J-8 Champion plugs in it, but after nine years the motor began to go through them quite regularly — it would quit running until I installed a new set of plugs. So I wrote to the Universal people and they suggested that I use hotter plugs, J-11s. Since I switched, a set of plugs lasts all season.

• *Alternator belt.* If you heard a squeak when you accelerated the engine last season, it probably came from a loose alternator belt. If you can turn the alternator pulley while the belt is in place, the belt is not tight enough. Ease off the nuts where the alternator is fastened to the block, loosen the ones on the brace below it, take the slack out of the belt, and retighten. The belt must not be rod-tight, but the pulley shouldn't slip. If the belt has become polished from long use and much slipping, it should be replaced with a new one.

• *Fuel filter.* Take that plug out of the bottom of the filter again, open the fuel shutoff, and catch some gas as it comes out. Drain any water that may be there, shut off the gas, and replace the plug. My plug is not brass or bronze, so I use a little Rectorseal No. 5 pipe compound on it.

• *Fuel pump.* Work the heavy wire loop that is under the fuel pump. This operates the pump and fills the carburetor with gas. (Of course you will have had to open the gas shutoff again to do this.)

• Look for leaks.

• *Water pump.* While you're back there with the motor, fill the grease cup on the water pump with waterproof grease and give the cup a turn. (If you have a rubber impeller pump, however, there won't be a grease cup.)

• Remove the plug that keeps the birds out of the end of the exhaust pipe during the winter, hook up the battery, make sure the transmission is in neutral, and start the engine. After it runs long enough to be convincing, shut it down and then replace the belt and pulley on the raw-water pump. The motor doesn't need to be started again until the boat is in the water.

MOTOR (Raw Water Cooled)

• If the water pump on the engine is a gear pump that has a grease cup, you can run the motor dry. If it is one that has a rubber impeller, it shouldn't be run dry, because the pump needs to be lubricated with water. In either case, the pump has been drained for the winter. Insert the plug in the opening under the gear pump. Tighten the plate at the back of the impeller pump.

• *Other plugs.* Check and replace if necessary: one plug near the after end of the manifold, one underneath the muffler. Some boats have an exhaust stack with a drain plug in it. There is probably a block drain somewhere under the alternator or behind the starter. Is there a plug in your oil cooler?

• *Oil change.* I usually change the oil after running the boat home, since by then the oil is good and hot and any sludge has been stirred up. As for the type of oil to use, each of the two widely different makes of engine I have used had a plate fastened to the transmission cover listing, among other things, the manufacturer's recommendation of a brand and weight of oil to be used in his product. Both engines required the same oil. Check your transmission plate. We add maybe half a cup of oil during a season.

SEACOCKS

Check all seacocks. You may have to squirt some oil or WD-40 through the through-hull fittings. Seacocks usually have one or two small plugs in them that can be removed for adding oil. Gate valves sometimes need a squirt of oil on their stems at the packing nut. If lubrication was done well in the fall, they should all work, but it is best to double-check in the spring.

THE HEAD

Replace the plug, pour some Aqualube or Sealube into the bowl, and work the valve and pump handle. If you have an MSD, follow the manufacturer's directions.

FRESHWATER LINES

Reattach freshwater lines.

FIBERGLASS HULL — Topsides and Decks

The last year or so, we've washed down topsides and decks with Fantastik. Any stubborn spots can be scrubbed with some nonabrasive powder such as Bon Ami. Don't use a tough scouring powder. We finish off by rubbing on a coat of good boat wax. Some kinds of car wax tend to leave a yellowish tint on a white hull. If we get around to it, we treat the cabin sides the same way. Of course we only wash the decks — we don't want to slip on them. (With all this "we" stuff, you can see one reason why I dedicated this tome to my wife, Ruth.)

Faded topsides or gelcoat that has a chalky film needs to be treated with a fine grade of rubbing compound, either by hand or with a power buffer. Don't use a heavy, abrasive compound — the gelcoat is thin. Finish off with a good paste wax.

To repair nicks and scratches in gelcoat, contact the manufacturer for a small can of gelcoat the same color as your boat. You will also need a very small amount of hardener. Do the repair before you wax the hull. Into a can lid pour a pool of gelcoat about the size of a 50-cent piece. Into this stir *two drops* of hardener. Work this into the blemish with a sharp knife point and build it up about $\frac{1}{16}$ inch above the surrounding level. Make sure that there are no trapped bubbles under it. Cover the patched area with a small square of cellophane or waxed paper and leave it overnight. Remove the covering and sand the patch with wet and dry #220 paper. Use the paper wet. Then go over it with #600 wet paper. Wash, buff with light rubbing compound, wash again. If the patch has shrunk somewhat, repeat the process. Give it a final coat of wax. A closed can of gelcoat that is kept in the refrigerator will probably last through the next season.

FIBERGLASS HULL — The Bottom

Remember that bottom paint is poisonous. Wear a good face mask and stand upwind when you sand it. The smoothness of the bottom is your business — it all depends on whether or not you are going in for racing. I content myself with going over the old soft paint with a stainless steel wire brush and a little work with garnet paper where it seems called for.

I have found one disadvantage in hauling out a keel-centerboarder on a cradle: I haven't seen my board for nine years. In the old days, when she would be hanging in the slings, I could crank the board down for sanding and painting. Now, the best I can do is to reach up into the slot with narrow pieces of wooden shingle that have strips of garnet paper glued to both faces. With the board hung up high so it doesn't rest on the sleepers, I can work these shingles up into the slot and knock out the young mussels and sand the surfaces somewhat.

Paint is applied with another piece of shingle that has strips cut from a paint roller refill glued on both sides. I'm not proud of this solution, but the board still goes up and down — and the boat comes out each fall without much of a wig hanging down from the slot.

Rolling the bottom paint on is faster than brushing, but not much smoother, and it does require quite a bit more of that expensive paint. Read the directions on the paint can to see what application method the manufacturer suggests. One boating season will probably indicate whether or not one coat is sufficient in your waters.

Some of your hot-shot boating friends may scream about this cavalier treatment of a boat's bottom, and they're probably right. Just tell them that it's what one fellow does after spending 18 years with the same bottom. It's still done with affection.

I use masking tape to cut in the waterline, and I used to mask off the deck when finishing something adjacent to it. However, it is almost impossible to remove the tape left on a fiberglass deck overnight when there is a rain or heavy dew, so I now do without the tape wherever possible.

Fittings of chrome, stainless steel, and so on, should be washed and sprayed, rubbed, or polished with something that will preserve their beauty. Any metal device that turns, screws, or slides should be lubricated with oil or grease so it will continue to do what it's supposed to do. Lubrication is especially important around salt water. Without it, a bronze set screw holding an aluminum ventilator in its aluminum frame may freeze up and twist off rather than turn the next time it's manipulated.

FIBERGLASS HULL — Brightwork

I chose mahogany for my brightwork, and, as a result, have some sanding and varnishing to do. I used to put the boat in the water and then do the work by dinghy — an elbow hooked over the rail, one hand holding a metal paint guard and the other wielding the brush. Not too bad until a breeze comes up — as it always does. Now I set up staging and do the job on land. If two coats are to be applied, I try to sand off two old coats to prevent a buildup.

I've never found a paint and varnish remover that won't also eat into gelcoat, and that's a problem when you try to strip something on a fiberglass boat. My varnished mahogany coaming finally began to blister, so I sanded, scraped, and worked it down as well as possible — and put on semigloss white paint. The next owner can strip it if he wants to.

This talk of varnished mahogany on a fiberglass boat is largely academic, because very few fiberglass hulls are finished off that way, although it does look nice.

Teak

One afternoon about 20 years ago a friend called me over to see something on his boat. He'd been hard at work on the teak in his cockpit and had finally finished. There it lay, a large area gleaming softly in its pristine beauty, just ready to suck up a bit of oil, grease, or dirt from a careless footstep. I was almost afraid to go aboard, but after carefully wiping my shoe soles on my pant legs, I did cross over —

the better to help him admire his handiwork. As I was leaving, I met the first of his afternoon guests at the head of his dock — her arms were loaded with goodies, which included a bag of potato chips. I'll lay money on it that there was one lady who didn't get to open her chips that afternoon.

Today it's a different matter altogether, because new products make teak much easier to care for. To generalize: the different teak products on the market come in two categories — cleaners and sealers.

Cleaners

Cleaners are easy to use, noncaustic, and won't harm marine paint, varnish, hardware, or seam filler. Some kinds are scrubbed and flushed off. They restore teak to the original golden color without bleaching. They do away with the dirty grey color and remove grease, oil, and food stains. Some kinds don't require scrubbing; they are poured on and hosed off. There is at least one cleaner that comes in a cream form that will stay where you put it, such as on overhead trim.

All cleaners prepare the wood for sealers.

Sealers

Sealers protect the teak from grease, oil, and food stains. They will not harm seam filler, paint, hardware, or varnish. There is also teak oil (a blend of natural oils), which waterproofs, preserves, and seals. I've seen teak that was varnished after it was cleaned or before it became dirty, and it looked elegant.

In summary, then, first you clean and then you seal. How do you decide which products to use? Talk to a marine paint dealer or someone like that. Tell him how much teak you have on your boat, what shape it's in, and so on. Ask around.

Of course it is possible to do nothing at all, but, in my opinion, in time the teak will look like the wood in a dirty old barnyard fence.

WOODEN HULL — The Bottom

When painting a wooden hull, as with many jobs, it's not a bad idea to start at the bottom and work upward. Assuming that the boat is carvel-built (smooth planked), the first consideration will be to determine the condition of the seams. Any compound that extends out in ridges must be scraped and sanded flush. Compound that is very hard and brittle should probably be replaced. (If chips and chunks fall out when poked with a tool, it is time to replace the compound.)

Find a rather large, flat, old file, heat the tang, and bend it into a hook. Grind it so the edge and the sides of the hook are sharp. (A good bit of tape wrapped around the file will save some blisters.) By using a hooking and prying motion, dig out the old compound and clean it from the edges of the planks. Do not go in deep enough to disturb the cotton, although it is good to inspect it here and there. Cotton has lost its life if it comes out in grey, dusty fibers rather than long, twisted strands. If you find much of the grey-fiber stuff, you need a recaulking job, and that's one for the professionals. We'll assume your boat is in better shape than that.

After you have hooked old putty out of the seams, you need to pay them. This consists of applying some thinned paint to the exposed face of the cotton and the edges of the planks with a paying brush, or, if you can't get one, a thin one-inch brush with the bristles trimmed short. Paying helps the seam compound stick and retards its drying out.

After the paint has dried, the new seam compound can be troweled or gunned in. Use a putty knife to work it well in, cut off the excess, and then channel each seam by drawing a round tool along it. One device that works for this is a headless spike driven into the end of a piece of broomstick and then curved. Trim off whatever is squeezed out.

A day later the bottom can be sanded and a coat of paint can be brushed on. If the bottom is pretty well dried out and open, it might not be a bad idea to spray the bilge with a hose from time to time.

In the enviable situation that the bottom of your wooden boat is in excellent condition, it will not need the above-mentioned hooking, recaulking, paying, seam filling, and so forth. Sanding and painting will suffice. Even so, when put over, it may take in quite a bit of water for a while, since the planking will have dried out. Here is one account of a solution to that problem:

My son Jim's Ostkust tends to leak like a sieve when he first puts her in, so to prevent that, he fills the underwater seams with Fels Naphtha soap after the bottom paint has dried and just before she is to be launched. The soap prevents leaking, and as planks swell and seams close up, the soap is squeezed out and it dissolves in the water. Jim says you have to use Fels Naphtha; one year he tried that kind in one side and another soap in the other. The side with the other soap began leaking almost at once.

WOODEN HULL — Topsides and Decks

Wash, let dry, then sand. I believe that if a hull is sanded enough each spring to take off a layer of old paint equal to the amount you plan to put on, it will become more beautiful, won't get heavier, and will not require stripping or burning off.

If there are light dents that you would like to fill, you can do that with a broad knife and a can of trowel cement. Dents through the paint and into the wood should be painted first. Place a blob of cement on a board that has a good sharp edge for cleaning the knife, cut off a little chunk of the cement with the broad knife, and make a single pass over the dent, leaving as little excess as possible. It dries hard and sands slowly. If you try a second pass, the cement will be roughened and one edge may pull away from the dent. For deep spots, successive layers can be applied as the cement dries. In an hour or so, you should be able to sand the stuff.

Wipe off the dust with a cloth dampened with turpentine, and flow on the paint with a good brush. Marine paint does not lend itself to much brushing out. It's nice to be in sunlight so you can see what you're doing, but hot sunshine will cause the paint to set up fast and show the laps. Don't worry about tiny insects — after the paint sets, they will brush off with hardly a trace.

One coat of paint or two? That depends on how you think the job looks after the first one. The more you put on, the more you should sand off later.

The next job will be to sand and paint the inside of the rail, the cabin sides, the coaming, and the cockpit. On second thought, you'd better do the varnishing next. It's easier to paint up to varnish than to varnish down to new paint. If the deck is canvas-covered, it will need sanding and then a coat of paint. Try to keep the paint to a minimum, since deck paint is very hard and too much of it, over a period of years, will result in cracking and blistering. If you have ever had to strip a deck, you'll know that it is an awful job that requires gallons of remover.

WOODEN HULL — Brightwork

Now back to that varnishing. Sand with a fine grade of garnet paper, wipe off the dust with a tack cloth (wetted with turpentine), then go over the wood with the palm of your hand. This will pick up most of the dust. Use a good brush and the best varnish you can find. After all the careful preparation and application, you want the job to last. For old work, I think that two coats should be a minimum. Read the label on the can to see what the manufacturer suggests.

A word about stripping off old paint and varnish versus burning it off. With varnish, never burn; you would be sure to char the wood. Remember that skill is required for this job. It is easy to char the wood and very easy to dig in with the scraping tool and raise splinters or make a gouge in the wood. It doesn't help if the boat is out in the wind when being worked on with a torch.

This past spring I stripped and repainted my little plywood dinghy, for the first time in about 10 years. I stripped part of the bottom with remover, and that went pretty slowly. Then I moved into the garage out of the wind and burned off the rest of the paint. Since the surface was flat, I could use a broad knife, after heating the paint with a propane torch equipped with a flame spreader, and it went quite well. It was faster than stripping, but I wouldn't try it on a round-bottomed hull.

Using paint remover, my cousin and I stripped one side of a 26-foot cruiser in just over two hours. Our procedure was as follows: The first fellow flowed remover with a brush on a 3- or 4-foot section at the bow and then waited for it to do its work; he added more remover from time to time. When it seemed to have quit acting, the second man used a scraper to remove the loose paint. While this was going on, a second area was treated with remover, and then more was brushed onto the first area. It may take three doses to do this, but in time the paint is wet down to the wood. Before it had time to dry, operator number 2 took a wad of coarse steel wool dipped in hot soapsuds and, working with the grain, scrubbed off the remaining paint and remover. (Half a pail of hot water with a handful of laundry detergent or TSP [trisodium phosphate] thrown in would be about right. If you use plenty of soapsuds, you'll get down to smooth and clean wood.) Next, with clean water, we flushed off all the soap and particles of steel wool. When the entire side was finished and the wood had become dry, we went over it with a rag saturated with turpentine. This will kill any remover that the soap didn't get out of the wood. Otherwise, there may be spots where the paint or, more especially, varnish will not set up. Gasoline works equally well, but for safety reasons, I don't recommend that.

Varnish can be stripped the same way, and it usually comes off more easily than paint. After stripping a varnished surface, such as a transom, be sure to wash it well and use the turpentine. After the area dries, sand it with fine garnet paper, wipe it, and then apply filler stain. Don't use thin oil stain. Put on the filler stain with a stiff brush, working with and across the grain. A little while before it dries (not long, though), rub it off with something coarse like burlap. Scrub hard. Finish off by rubbing briskly with the grain, using an old bath towel. It will take a polish that looks elegant. It later fades, but don't worry about that. Cover it to protect it from the weather, and let it dry at least overnight. A thin coat of varnish, followed by three or four others, with light sanding and careful wiping between, and you will have something that really gleams.

I've seen older reconditioned boats on which the owner painted the deck hardware with aluminum paint. My personal reaction: It looks dreadful. Aluminum does not look like galvanizing, and it certainly doesn't look like chrome. I'd rather see the hardware painted the same color (although a darker shade) as the deck. In that connection, I've always thought that buff was the proper color for a white-hulled sailboat's deck. But don't let me influence you.

Last chore: Put on a second coat of bottom paint and cut in the waterline.

Last word of advice: Don't forget the bilge plug.

Appendix A

A Proper Mooring Pendant

I think it is safe to say that the part of a mooring system that may be the first to let go in a storm is not the mushroom, the chain, a swivel or shackle. It's the mooring pendant where it rubs and chafes as it goes over the bow chock. This is especially true of nylon line, since that material has a low resistance to chafe.

My son writes that one fall four of his fellow club members lost boats in a blow — on each one the pendant had chafed through. The bill to lift them back off the salt flats was well over $300 each. In many areas the owners would have been lucky indeed to have their boats come to rest on only salt flats.

After selecting line of the proper size, it takes only a little time and effort to make it into a pendant that will be quite safe to use.

LENGTH

Piloting, Seamanship and Small Boat Handling recommends a pendant length 2½ times the height of your bow above water. With 3-foot freeboard forward, you should have a pendant 7½ to 8 feet from eyesplice to eyesplice. Other references suggest a pendant length equal to a third of your boat's overall length. I prefer that recommendation, because it allows you a little more latitude when attempting to moor with a sea making up.

DIAMETER

Select the largest-diameter nylon line that will pass easily between the horns of your bow chock *after* it has been served with marlin and fitted with an anti-chafe sleeve, as will be described below. I am able to use ¾-inch nylon.

TREATMENT

Splicing

As the first photo in this series shows, at one end of the pendant there should be an eye spliced tightly around the proper-size thimble. When making a splice in synthetic material, there should be five tucks to each strand, rather than the three that are sufficient in manila. There is a seizing of waxed synthetic small stuff around the sides of the thimble and the line. In case the eye stretches and opens somewhat, the seizing will keep the thimble in place. This end of the pendant is the one that will be shackled to the chain at the mooring float.

The eyesplice at the inboard end of the pendant is a long one — long enough to be tucked through the opening of an open-based cleat and then looped around its horns.

The eyesplice and thimble on the outboard end of the mooring pendant. The start of the serving also shows.

In the case of a cleat that is not open-based, a short line can be tied around the throat of the splice and then made fast to the cleat.

Serving

I had one pendant that became twisted so that the strands became unlaid and formed a hockle (which I couldn't work out). I now serve the pendant with marlin, which prevents twisting and unlaying.

Beginning to serve the pendant with marlin. The serving mallet is in place.

The old jingle goes:
Worm and parcel with the lay,
Turn and serve the other way.

I do not worm (wind small stuff in the groove between strands) or parcel (wrap a continuous canvas bandage around the line), but I do serve, and I remember the ditty so I'll wrap the marlin in the proper direction. One large ball of marlin will serve 8 or 10 feet of ¾-inch line.

The gear shown in the photo was set up for demonstration purposes only. There is no eye spliced into the end of the line. Here's how:

1. Stretch the line between two trees and, with a handy billy or a boom vang at one end, put a lot of tension on it. The line should be at about elbow height or a little higher.

2. Start wrapping marlin tightly around the line and its own end. See the end of the marlin hanging down below the nylon in the picture? Wrap in the opposite direction (left) from the lay of the line (right). After a number of turns:

3. Use the serving mallet, which is a short-handled hard-wood mallet whose head is 6 inches long and 1½ inches in

diameter. A hollow runs along the head from end to end and opposite the handle. This keeps it from slipping off the line.

4. As shown, wrap two turns of marlin around the line and mallet, then around behind the handle and along the line to your first mate, who will hold the ball, keep tension on the marlin, and pass the ball around and around the nylon, keeping up with you as you twirl the mallet.

5. As you wind the mallet around and around, you keep tension on the marlin with your thumb and see to it that each turn is tight against the last one. Done properly, this results in a tight and polished serving. (You can see by the grooves worn in the mallet that respectable tension is possible.)

Time? An hour or so.

Next finish the serving at the other end. Hold the last turns of the serving tightly, get rid of the mallet, lay a pencil on and parallel to the nylon, loosely wind on 10 turns around the pencil and the nylon, cut off the ball, pull out the pencil, stick the end of the marlin through (under) the loops left by the pencil, wind the turns in order around as tightly as you can, and then pull the end of the marlin under those tight turns (with pliers) until you've taken up all the slack. Cut off the exposed portion.

LEATHER CHAFING SLEEVE

This is the most important part of the whole mooring gear. I buy moccasins from a shoemaker, and twice, upon request, he has given me a bag of thick leather scraps. He seemed interested in the use I intended for them.

The leather is cut to form a sleeve six inches or so long and just wide enough to be snug when laced. Holes are punched along the edges and the sleeve is laced around the pendant at a point where it will pass over the bow chock. I use a

Above: Leather chafing sleeve laced onto the served pendant at the location of the bow chock. Right: The moored boat with chafing gear in position.

length of waxed nylon whipping line threaded through a pair of small sail needles, one at either end. By a combination of shoelacing stitch and extra turns through opposite holes, the sleeve can be secured tightly. Since the leather gets wet in service and tends to loosen, the ends of the sleeve should be bound tightly with a number of turns of the whipping thread. This is to prevent the sleeve from slipping out of position on the chock. The fourth photo shows the pendant and its leather chafing gear in the boat's chock while it is riding to its mooring.

When a 35-knot no'thwester comes in at low tide and my boat and dink are separated by several hundred yards of mud flat so that I have *no* way of getting out there and she's pitching and tossing around just three or four boat's lengths to windward of ledges, I remind myself of that leather chafing gear and my level of anxiety drops a bit. You can be sure, though, that I make a thorough inspection when next aboard.

Appendix B

Engine Maintenance

Five motor illustrations and a wiring diagram are arranged here for easy reference. There are suggestions already made in the text as well as some additional ones.

THE ENGINE BOX HAS BEEN REMOVED

- 1. The pulley on the raw-water pump that is removed when the boat is laid up. It is not replaced until it has been launched. This keeps the impeller from being scored when it is dry.
- 2. The end of the heat exchanger where raw water enters from the pump. There are two plugs beneath the heat exchanger. The first plug drains raw water and is removed at layup and replaced during fitting-out. The other drains antifreeze and is not disturbed.
- 3. The arrow points to the plate at the rear of the raw-water pump that is loosened at haulout to drain the pump. It is re-secured at fitting-out time.
- 4. The heavy tubing that contains the centerboard pendant. There is a curved piece of aluminum taped to the back of this tube to prevent chafing by the pump belt, which is quite close to the tube.

THE ENGINE-ROOM BULKHEADS HAVE BEEN REMOVED

- 1. The top tank for the freshwater cooling system. This is kept nearly full of 50/50 water and antifreeze.
- 2. The alternator. Low down on the engine block behind the alternator is a cock to drain water from the block. On some engines, this is on the end of a protruding tube to make it more accessible. In motors that are freshwater cooled, this drain is not touched. In motors cooled by raw water and having no heat exchanger, this cock is opened in the fall and closed in the spring.
- 3. The approved marine-type fuel shutoff valve.
- 4. The fuel filter. Water and dirty gas separated out by the filter can be drained by unscrewing the plug at the bottom of the filter's bowl. I do this in the spring and the fall. Check the plug for any leaks.
    The flexible fuel line that goes to the motor's fuel pump can be seen running from the filter to the engine. I placed metal clamps on the metallic ends of this fuel line and connected them with a copper wire to make sure the entire fuel system was grounded. This reduces the danger of a spark when the fuel tank is being filled.
- 5. The end of the air line that runs to a cowl ventilator on the after deck of the boat. The cowl faces aft to draw out any fumes near the carburetor. Another air line nearby, which brings in air from a second ventilator, faces forward.
- 6. The forward end of the heat exchanger.

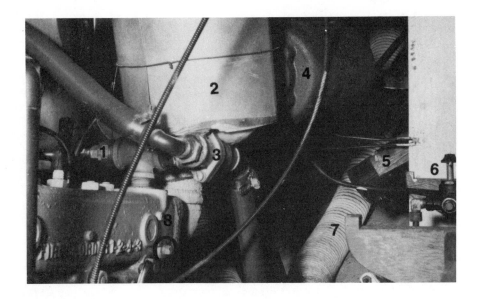

A CLOSE-UP OF THE PORT SIDE OF THE MOTOR

- 1. Engine water temperature sensor, which is wired to a gauge that reads in degrees Fahrenheit. When the gauge indicates a temperature much higher than 160 degrees, I know it's time to clean the raw-water screen, which means: shut down, close the raw-water seacock, open the screen chamber, remove the screen, and shake out weeds. Then reverse the procedure, and don't forget to close the seacock again.
- 2. Aluminum housing surrounds the insulation for the hot exhaust loop, which has no cooling water in it.
- 3. The thermostat allows engine water to circulate through a bypass until it heats up rapidly to 160 degrees, at which point it is directed in part or in entirety through the heat exchanger. Without the thermostat and bypass, the engine would warm up slowly, to the detriment of its valves and its efficiency.
- 4. The muffler. Unlike the exhaust stack, the muffler is water-cooled. On its under side is a drain plug that must be removed in the fall and replaced in the spring. This applies to both raw-water- and freshwater-cooled engines.
- 5. The open horn connected to a large CO_2 extinguisher, which is located in a cockpit locker where it could be activated instantly in case of an engine fire.
- 6. The approved fuel shutoff. This is down low, which means you have to get on your knees to open or close it. This brings your nose quite close to the area of possible gasoline drips, so you automatically are checking for leaks each time you turn the gas on or off.
- 7. The hose from one of the cowl ventilators.
- 8. The plug in the manifold. Remove and replace it in raw-water-cooled engines, leave it alone in freshwater-cooled motors.

MARINE ENGINE — STARBOARD SIDE

- 1. The raw-water pump. This will be found on freshwater-cooled engines, not on raw-water-cooled ones. It brings raw water in via a seacock, a strainer basket, and a hose and sends it through the heat exchanger. From there, the warmed water is discharged from the boat partially through the muffler and exhaust pipe and partially through a second pipe that goes to a through-hull in the transom.

   This pump is drained by backing off the machine screws at the back to loosen the round plate there. The pump should not be run dry.

- 2. The starting motor. This seldom needs any attention.

- 3. The starter solenoid. A light current initiated by pressing the starter button on the instrument panel causes a heavy-duty switch to close. This allows a heavy current to pass through the starting motor and thus turn the engine. Some solenoids have a thimble-shaped cap at the forward end covering a push button by which you can activate the starting motor while working on the engine.

- 4. The petcock that drains cooling water from the lowest part of the engine block. This may be difficult to locate on older engines, but it must be opened to drain the block on raw-water-cooled engines. On freshwater-cooled engines, it is not opened.

- 5. The motor-cooling water-circulating pump. In freshwater-cooled motors, this pump circulates water around the motor until it gets up to temperature and then through the heat exchanger as controlled by the thermostat. The pump need not be drained at the end of the season if the motor is filled with antifreeze.

   In raw-water-cooled engines, the pump brings in water from the outside and circulates it around the motor until it is up to temperature. Then the hot water is sent overboard via the muffler and exhaust pipe. In this case, when being laid up, the pump should be drained. A gear pump, as shown, is drained by removing the plug (number 7) beneath it. In the case of an impeller pump, it is drained by unscrewing machine bolts and backing off the plate, as described for the raw-water pump (number 1).

- 6. Water-pump grease cup, on a gear pump. It should be filled with a good grade of water-pump grease and should be turned down from time to time. (An impeller pump doesn't have such a grease cup.)

- 7. The drain plug at the bottom of the gear pump.

- 8. The ignition coil. It is often suggested that you carry a spare coil, and that's probably a good idea, but after seven years with one boat and 18 with another, I've never needed the spare.

- 9. The distributor. Wipe a little Vaseline on the faces of the shaft, drop a little light oil on the felt at the top of the shaft under the rotor, and squirt a few drops of #10 oil into the oil cup that takes care of the shaft bearing. It's important to keep the interior of the distributor dry. If necessary, mop it out with a paper towel and then spray it with WD-40. I keep a spare distributor cap, rotor, and set of points on the boat.

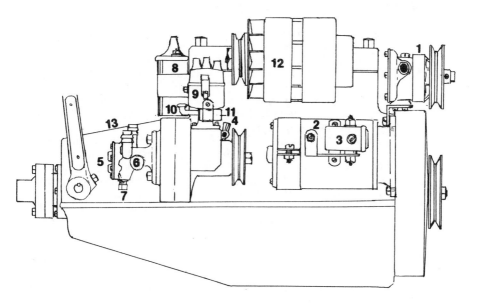

- 10. Distributor oil cup (see above).
- 11. Condenser. On some motors the condenser is inside the body of the distributor. It's good to carry a spare.
- 12. The alternator. On older motors there may be a generator instead of an alternator. Keep the belt rather tight. When an old belt becomes polished, replace it. The new one will soon stretch and need tightening. If there is a squeak when you accelerate, it probably indicates a loose alternator belt.
- 13. The manufacturer's name plate on the cover of the reverse gear housing. On some engines this plate lists the recommended brand and grade of oil.

MARINE ENGINE — PORT SIDE

- 1. The water-cooled exhaust manifold. Water enters from the engine-head at 1(A) and leaves at 1(B), where the thermostat is located. There is no water in the dry exhaust stack (number 3).
- 2. The plug by which water is drained from the exhaust manifold at layup time in the case of raw-water-cooled engines. In a freshwater-cooled engine, which has a heat exchanger, the plug would not be removed, since the cooling chambers of the engine would contain antifreeze.
- 3. The dry exhaust loop or stack. This arrangement ensures that any water in the muffler and exhaust pipe won't back up into the manifold and go from there via the exhaust valves to the cylinders, where it would be the cause of severe damage to the motor. It must be insulated to protect the surroundings from too much heat.
- 4. The plug by which water is drained from the muffler at the end of the season. This needs to be done no matter whether the motor is freshwater cooled or raw-water cooled.
- 5. The intake manifold to which the carburetor is connected.
- 6. The carburetor.
- 7. The throttle lever.
- 8. The screen on the flame arrestor. In case of an engine backfire, this screen absorbs heat from the burning air/gasoline mixture and extinguishes the flame before it leaves the carburetor so that any gasoline fumes will not be ignited. This flame-arrestor screen tends to collect lint, so reach in occasionally with an old toothbrush and wipe it off.
- 9. The choke lever, an aid in starting a cold engine. The lever is connected to a butterfly valve in the air horn by which you can diminish the volume of air entering the carburetor, thereby enriching the mixture of gas drawn into the engine cylinders.
- 10. Idle needle valve. If the engine idles erratically, adjust this valve one way or the other until it smooths up. If the valve is way out of adjustment, adjust it gradually by starting with one turn.
- 11. Main jet adjustment. The approximate setting is two and a half turns open. Turn it in (to the right) until the engine speed is reduced noticeably. Then slowly back it out until the engine runs smoothly. Too rich a mixture will cause fouled spark plugs and carbon buildup. A line of soot on the transom near the exhaust pipe opening is one indication of too rich a mixture.
- 12. Drain plug in the bottom of the carburetor bowl. It is a good idea to remove this plug at the beginning and end of each season to drain any dirty gas and sediment that may have accumulated in the bottom of the bowl.

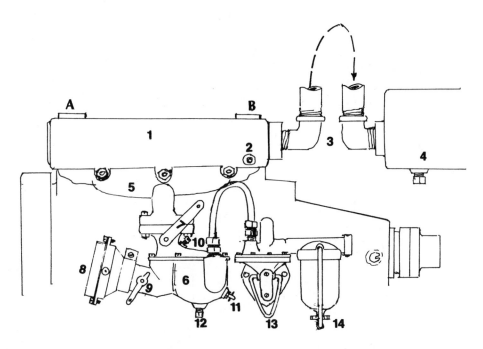

- 13. The fuel pump with its manual control by which you can pump gas into the carburetor of an engine that has not yet been started. It is wise to carry a spare fuel pump or a rebuilding kit on board.
- 14. The glass sediment bowl on the fuel pump. If you have an efficient fuel filter in the line ahead of the pump, you seldom will see sediment in this bowl, but it should be removed and cleaned at least once a season anyway. If this is not done, the tightening device at the bottom of the bowl, which keeps it securely in place, may rust on its threads, making eventual removal very difficult.

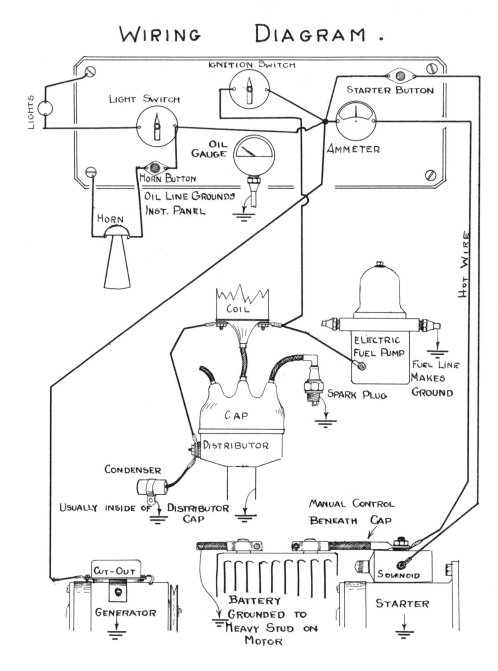

WIRING DIAGRAM.

WIRING DIAGRAM

I worked up this diagram for myself and later wired two boats by referring to it.

In the case of a nonmetallic instrument panel, a copper or brass grounding plate can be screwed to the back side of the panel. This should be drilled with a row of holes so that wires that need to be grounded can be fastened to it. The plate itself can be grounded to the copper tube that goes from the engine to the oil gauge.

To ground a wire to the plate, crimp a terminal to its end and fasten that with a round-headed brass screw that passes through a hole in the plate and into the wood beneath.

It is important to notice the way in which your battery was originally grounded in your boat. In some wiring systems the positive terminal is the one grounded to the motor, and in others, the negative terminal is grounded. Whichever way it was done, it should not be reversed.

Index

A-frame winter cover, 81-82
Air hammer/pile driver, 21
Air line, 114
Alidade: measuring for gin pole, 47
Alternator: tightening the belt, 93; mentioned, 114, 117
Aluminum paint, 104
Anchor fasteners, 73
Antifreeze, 93
Aqualube, 80, 95
Awning fittings as float bearings, 5

Barge, from float, 6, 29-38 *passim*
Battery: haulout removal, 78; during fitting out, 94; wiring, 121
Bilge plug, 104
Block, on float winch, 31

Bolo knife: to clean spruce, 13; to make gin pole, 47
Bolts. *See* Eyebolts; Ring bolts
Bottom: scrubbing, 75; painting, 75, 97; cleaning with sand and water, 76; fiberglass, 96-97; wooden, care of, 100-101
Bow chock, 105, 109
Brass pins, 6
Brightwork: care, 98; varnishing, 102-103
Bronze flange/bracket, as davit mount, 15
Bulkhead: setting pilings, 24; for deep water, high bank, 26-27; from steel boxcar panels, 28
Bulkheads, removed from engine room, 114
Buoy, mooring, 34
Butterboards, 66

123

Butterfly valve, 118
Bypass, engine, 115

Cable, in bulkhead construction, 28
Canvas, as winter cover material, 83
Carburetor, 118; air horn, 78
Carriage bolts, on float, 5
Casite, use during haulout, 78
Catwalk: float, 1, 4; anchored into ledge, 1, 11; need for hoisting device, 15; securing, 16
Centerboard pendant, 113
Chafing sleeve, 109
Chain yoke, 67
Channel iron, on cradle, 69
Chart storage, 86
Choke lever, 118
Cockpit drain, cover before storage, 80
Come-along, 69
Commercial marine railways, 66
Companionway doors, need for replacements during storage, 80
Condenser, 117
Cooling system, flushing during haulout, 76-77, 114
Cowl ventilator, 114, 115
Cradle: source of timbers, 18; construction details, 58-62 *passim;* importance of, 61; during haulout, 75, 97
Creosote: on dock, 20; to lengthen life of wood, 27; on gin pole, 41; for winter mast storage rack, 53, 62
Cribs, wooden, as wharf support, 23

Davit: rigging, 15; winch, 15
Deck: float planks, 3; fiberglass, maintenance of, 96; wooden, refinishing, 102
Dinghy, handling at float, 4
Distributor: during haulout, 78; during fitting out, 93, 116; oil cup, 117

Dockage (versus wharfage), 17
Docks, 17-26 *passim;* design for seasonal removal, 20; weather hazards, 21; installing with Jeep, 21; siting, 23; timbers for, 23; construction, 25-26
Dolly, mast and pole, 53
Downhaul, 53
Drain: used during haulout, 77-79; cockpit, 80; plug, replaced when fitting out, 93, 115-116
Drawknife, 13, 47
Drill bit, sharpening on "greenstone," 12
Drilling into ledge, 12

Engine: draining during haulout, 78; rust during storage, 79; maintenance, 112-121 *passim;* box removed, 113; speed adjustments, 118; wiring, 121
Exhaust: pipe, attention to during haulout, 83; pipe, during fitting out, 94; loop and stack, 94, 115, 116, 118; manifold, 118
Eye band, for gin pole, 47
Eyebolts: on float, 4, 10, 11; drop-forged vs. cast, 11; regular or shoulder style, 11; set into ledge, 12; on dock fender board, 26
Eye-straps, at steering pulleys on float, 6

Face piece/fender board, 9
Fantastik, 92, 95
Fasteners, 70, 73. *See also* Eyebolts
Fels Naphtha, to prevent hull seam leaks, 101
Fender: on float, 5, 9; fender board on dock, 25-26; homemade, 90
Fiberglass: attention to during fitting out, 95-97 *passim;* precautions when sanding, 96-97

Filler stain, 103, 104
Fire extinguisher, 115
Fire hose, use in dock construction, 25-26
"Fisherman's red" bottom paint, 75-76
Fitting out, 92-104 *passim*
Fittings, care of, 97
Flame arrestor screen, 118
Float: size, 2; uses of, 2, 4, 5, 6, 29; hardware, 4, 5; materials, 5, 6; stability of, 5, 14; siting of, 10; haulout procedure, 43
Flushing cooling system, 76-77
Free-spooling winch, for mast-stepping gin pole, 48
Freshwater: system, 79, 114; lines, 95
Fuel: filter, 78, 94, 114; line, 114; pump, 94, 119; shutoff valve, 114, 115

Garnet paper, 97, 102, 103. *See also* Sanding
Gasoline: system, attention during haulout, 78-79; full vs. empty tank during storage, 79; as paint remover, 103
Gate valves, 95
Gelcoat, 96, 98
Gin pole, 39-45 *passim;* maintenance of, 41; load capability, 41; mast-stepping, 47, 74; winter storage of, 74
"Greenstone" sharpener, 12

Hanger bolts, for topping lift, 48
Happy Parrot (vessel), 84, 85
Hatch covers, 80
Haulout (and winterizing), 75-84 *passim*
Head: winterizing, 80; fitting out, 95
Heat exchanger: draining during haulout, 77; fitting-out procedure, 93; mentioned, 113, 115, 116
Hockle, in mooring pendant, 107
Hoists: for catwalk, 15; for mast, 57

Hooks, to lift mooring, 30
Horse trailer, converted to boat trailer, 65
Hydraulics, setting pilings with, 22

Idle needle valve, 118
Ignition coil, 116
Impeller pump, 94, 113
Insulation for exhaust, 115
Intake manifold, 118

Lead around eyebolts, 11-12
Leaks, prevention of, 101
Leather chafing sleeve, 109
Line: poly, 48, 69; storing anchor, 80; nylon, 105, 111
Lobster well, in float, 3, 4, 6
Locker covers, 92
Locust cleats, for gin-pole side guys, 47
Lubrication: Aqualube, 80, 95; Sealube, 95; during fitting out, 97-98

Maintenance, seasonal schedule of, 83-84
Manifold: plug, 115, 118; intake, 118
Manila: for second topping lift, 48; for side guys, 51
Marine railways, 66
Marlin: for mooring pendant, 107; wrapping technique, 108
Masonite, 48
Mast: pole size, 47; raising, 51; lifting, 53; and pole dolly, 53; stepping, unstepping manpower, 53; handling, 56, 57; winter storage, 74
Mildew, prevention during storage, 80
Mooring: float, 1; siting, 10; buoy, 34; lowering, 34; setup, 34; materials and construction, 37, 38; pendant, 105; leather chafing sleeve, 109
Motor: to convert float into barge, 6, 33; steering mechanism for, 33; motor

tune, use during haulout, 78; checklist for fitting out, 93

MSD (marine sanitation device), 90

Muffler: draining during haulout, 77; attention when fitting out, 93; mentioned, 115, 116, 118

Nylon: mast-lifting strop, 53; line, 105, 111

Oil change, 95

Painting: bottom, 75; fiberglass hull, 97; wooden hull, 100-102; and varnishing, 102; stripping vs. burning off oil finish, 102-103; aluminum paint, 104

Pendant, mooring, 105-111 *passim*

"Penta" (Pentachlorophenol), 6, 13

Petcock, 116

Pier, made from old materials, 18

Pile driver, hand-held, 21

Pilings, setting into soft bottom, 22

Pipe compound, 93, 94

Plastic piping, on float, 5

Plugs, 94

"Plumber's furnace" to melt lead, 12

Polyethylene, as winter cover material, 83

Polypropylene: on winch, 48; during launching, 69

Polyurethane foam, in mooring float, 37

Potwarp, on catwalk, 13, 14

Preservatives, 6

Pumps: bicycle, 12; raw-water, 77, 93, 113, 116; water, 94, 116; impeller, 116; gear, 116

Railway: commercial marine, 66; home-built, 67-73 *passim*

Ratchet winch, for stepping mast, 47

Raw-water: pump. *See* Pumps; screen, 115

Rectorseal. *See* Pipe compound

Ridgepole, 81-83 *passim*

Ring bolts, 51

Ring plate: for float, 4; for gin pole, 47

Rode, anchor. *See* Anchor lines

Rubbing compound, 96

Salt water, as preservative, 6

Sanding: precautions, 96, 97; using home-made shingle, 97; importance of regular, 101; when refinishing, 101-103 *passim*

Scouring powder, 96

Screen: raw-water, 115; flame arrestor, 118

Scrubber, home-made, for bottom, 76

Seacocks, 95, 115

Sealube. *See* Lubrication

Seams, in wooden hull, 100

Serving mallet, 108, 109

Side guys, 51, 57

Sleeve, leather chafing, 109

Spark plugs, 93, 118

Spar tree, 46

Stanchions, 81

Staples, on float, 9

Starter solenoid, 116

Steel: for railway, 68, 69; in railway fittings, 73

Steering pulleys, on float, 6

Stern rail, 81

Storage: rack for mast, 53, 86; facilities, 85-91 *passim;* boat shed, 86; garage, 86; bosun's locker, 86; for charts, 86, 89; sail and gear, 91; dinghy, 91; combined with workroom, 91

Strap iron braces, for cradle, 60, 61

Stripping paint and varnish, 102-103

Styrofoam: log for float, 3; for mooring float, 37

Teak, care of, 99

Thermostat, engine, 115, 118
Throttle lever, 118
Tie-downs, on winter cover, 83
Tiller, during storage, 81
Tools, security during storage, 80
Topping lift: 47, 48; second, 48
Topsides: fiberglass, 95, 96; wooden, 101, 102
Towing eye, on butterboard, 66
Tractor, as float winch, 43
Trailer: cradle, 62; construction specifications, 62; four-wheel nontandem, 64; four-wheel tandem, 65
Transducer, cleaning during haulout, 76
Travelift, 62
Tripod, construction of, for float, 29
TSP (trisodium phosphate), 103
Turpentine, 101, 102, 103

U.S. Army Corps of Engineers, 23

Valve: gate, 95; fuel shutoff, 114, 115; idle needle, 118

Varnish, 102, 103
Vaseline, 48, 93, 116
Ventilation: in storage areas, 80; under winter cover, 82, 114

WD-40: on mast before storage, 74; on bottom valves, 76; on distributor and cap, 78, 93; during fitting out, 95
Water: salt-, as preservative, 6; pump, 94, 116; temperature sensor, 115
Wedges, cradle, 75
Wharfage, 17; wharf support, 23
White Cap (vessel), 18, 56
Winch: davit, 15; in lifting float/barge, 30, 31; ratchet, 47; free-spooling, 48; worm-gear, 69
Winter cover: 53; frame, 81, 82; size and materials, 83
Wiring, engine, 121
Worming and parceling, 108

Yard access, 67

ABOUT THE AUTHOR

When Howard Barnes retired in 1971
after 38 years as a high school science
teacher in Ohio, he was finally able to
devote his energies to his lifelong in-
terest in boats. His Tartan 27, *Happy
Parrot* (which he finished off himself), is
the most recent of his craft, which have
included a sailing canoe, an old Maine-
built gaff-rigger, a Gar Wood ex-rumrunner, and a Seagull sloop. He is a permanent member of the U.S. Coast
Guard Auxiliary and a life member of
the U.S. Power Squadrons. His nick-
name, "Dry Rot" Barnes, comes from his
earlier book, *Your Boat, Its Selection
and Care*, published in 1948. Barnes and
his wife, Ruth, now live in a house they
built on the Maine coast.